# Calling
# Upon
# the Name
# of the Lord

Bill Freeman

*Ministry Publications*

*Scottsdale, Arizona*

Library of Congress Catalog
Card Number: 94-75760

ISBN 0-914271-59-8

*Ministry Publications*

PO Box 48255
Spokane, WA 99228
(509) 466-4777 / (800) 573-4105
Email: ministry@thechristian.org
www.thechristian.org

Printed in the United States of America

Patti & Roy Roberts
CBC-NYC 2006

# Contents

# 1 ❯ The Significance of the Name of Jesus

The entire universe has a destiny with the name of Jesus. We cannot ignore, reject, neglect, or be indifferent to anything related to that name. Not one of us can say, "That's not for me." Let me announce to you, you have a destiny with the name of Jesus. Philippians 2:9-11 tells us that at the name of Jesus every knee will bow and every tongue will confess that Jesus Christ is Lord, to the glory of God the Father. So we all have a destiny with that name. We need to apprehend, appreciate, and understand the significance and the reality of the name of Jesus because God has highly exalted this name. It is more excellent than any other name. It is higher than the angels, higher than any other lord or dominion or rule. The name of Jesus is the highest name.

### *The name of Jesus and Jesus Himself*

When we read the Gospels we may have a kind of secret admiration for those who were with the Lord Jesus during the days of His flesh. We may wish that we could have been there too. What would it have been like to walk down a road and actually be able to see and contact Christ — to be so close to Him that if you had a need you could follow the crowd and press through to touch the hem of His garment! We may consider the people who lived with Christ in the flesh to be more favored or privileged than we are. Yet the Bible reveals that "Jesus Christ is *the same* yesterday, today, and forever" (Heb. 13:8). But you ask, how is He the same? In what way is He the same to me as He was to those living 2000 years ago? The answer is simple. It is in His name. He is the same in the realm of His name.

Calling on the name of Jesus is the same as being present with Jesus in the flesh. In fact, it is better. Why? In the flesh, Christ was limited in His availability to men; but now in resurrection He is available to all as the Spirit (2 Cor. 3:17). His availability in resurrection as the Spirit is as near as the mention of His name (1 Cor. 6:11). Christ is touchable all the time, in any place, under any circumstance, and through any environment. Regardless of your condition — if you are emotionally on the floor, even if you have made your bed in hell — you can open your mouth and say "Jesus," and He is there. "No one can say, Jesus is Lord! except in the Holy Spirit" (1 Cor. 12:3).

We can experience our precious Lord Jesus in a direct way by calling upon His name. The Lord comes to us in His name. Isaiah 52:6 says, "Therefore My people shall know My name; therefore they shall know in that day that I am He who speaks: Behold, it is I." When we speak His name, His response is, "Behold, it is I." And Romans 10:12 declares, "The same Lord of all is rich unto all who call upon Him." The Lord Himself with all His riches becomes our portion and experience when we call upon Him. So it is imperative for us as believers to see the significance of the name of Jesus, to see from the divine point of view the deep meaning of the precious name of Jesus, and to appreciate the revelation of His name given to us in the Word. It is the name that is above every name — the name that in this universe has a value beyond what we could imagine.

## THE SIGNIFICANCE OF NAMES IN THE BIBLE

To deepen our appreciation of the name of Jesus we need to understand the significance of names in the Bible. That is, what is the meaning behind a name according to the Bible's concept? In Scripture, are names merely given because they rhyme or sound pleasant to the ear? A careful study of Scripture reveals that when names were given, they were not given in a meaningless or indiscriminate way. The Bible's way of naming was not like today's way of naming, where you peruse a name book and choose the name that sounds the best. The practice of naming in the Bible was always based upon the character, nature, and destiny of a person. The name was a summary of something in a person's character, calling, and history. To know the name of a person was to know something about that person's history and makeup.

## *The name stands for the person*

In the Bible a name always represented a person. The name stood for the person. This is the significance of a name in the Bible. For example, Acts 1:15 says, "And in those days Peter stood up in the midst of the brothers (altogether the number of *names* was about a hundred and twenty)." In this verse to speak of the number of *names* is to speak of the number of *persons*. In other words, the name is equal to the person. This is the basic concept of a name in the Bible.

Revelation 3:4 also shows us that the name stands for the person: "But you have a few *names* in Sardis who have not defiled their garments, and they will walk with Me in white because they are worthy." Here the Holy Spirit uses the word "names" to signify the persons. There were a few names in Sardis who were obviously the few overcoming persons in that church. So we see again that a name and a person are interchangeable in the Bible. Names were not meaningless labels; names matched the particular persons. This is significant in appreciating the name of Jesus. The name of Jesus *is* the person of Jesus. So when we say "Jesus," we are touching the person of Jesus. That name is His Person, and that name has been given to us to speak anytime, anywhere, in any environment, that we might enjoy and experience His Person and all that He is. This is profound, yet so simple. Everything is in this one name — Jesus.

### To know the name is to know the person

Not only does the name stand for the person, but to know the name is to know the person. First Samuel 25:25 says, "Please, let not my lord regard this scoundrel Nabal. For as his name is, so is he: Nabal [Fool] is his name, and folly is with him." This example is negative, but its principle is true of names in the Bible: "As his name is, so is he." When we put the name of Jesus into this phrase, it would read, "As His name is [Jesus], so is He." And Matthew 1:21 tells us the significance of that name: "You shall call His name JESUS, for He will save His people from their sins." So when we say "Jesus," we are touching a Person who saves us. He is saving us from our sins. As His name is, so we know Him as our Savior God. The revelation of Himself is in His name.

Psalm 9:10 reveals the same truth: "And those who know Your name will put their trust in You." Knowing the name and knowing the Lord Himself issues in putting our trust in Him. Knowing His name and knowing Himself go together. The simple, practical way to know the Lord is in His name. Confessing the name "Jesus" is the most profound thing you can do in your spiritual life, because that name puts you in direct contact with Him.

Calling upon His name brings us out of merely thinking about Jesus or wishing to be more like Jesus. It brings us out of our emotions and our powerless desires to be like Him. Calling brings us out of our searching and endless seeking. Just by speaking His name we are instantly transferred into a participation in His Person.

Not only are we transferred by the name of Jesus, but the entire universe is being consummated in the name of Jesus. In this consummation the Lord is heading up all things in the heavens and on the earth. All things will be brought to their peak for one grand finale — that at the name of Jesus every knee will bow and every tongue will "confess out" (lit.) that Jesus Christ is Lord, to the glory of God the Father.

The whole universe is going to be reduced to the utter simplicity and confession of the name of Jesus and to the acknowledgment that that name is above every name — that Jesus is Lord. The name that has been cursed, the name that is taken in vain, the name that has been trampled in the streets, the name that has been profaned by the enemy — that same name is now in the process of being sanctified. Through our lips today in the church, that name is sanctified, and one day all will acknowledge the name and majesty of Jesus. Hallelujah! What a name!

*The name expresses the nature of a thing or person*

Even in the beginning when Adam named the animals, the naming was according to the nature of the animal (Gen. 2:19-20). The Lord had Adam identify all these living creatures by a name that was fitting to their nature. He brought all the animals to Adam, and Adam discerned their nature and named them accordingly. He looked at one of the creatures and said, "This is a cow. This big creature expresses cow life." No name is so fitting to a cow as "cow." Then another animal came, and Adam said, "This is a horse." Again, the name "horse" accurately depicts the nature of that animal. Then the Lord brought a flying creature to Adam, and Adam said, "This is a bird." Adam gave names to all the fowl of the air. It is instructive to see that the naming of the animals was done according to their nature.

What happened with the animals also took place with the naming of Adam's wife. Adam named his wife Eve (Heb. *life* or *living*) because she was "the mother of all living" (Gen. 3:20). Her name, Eve, expressed her nature and function. Thus, we see the Biblical concept behind the naming of animals and humans. The name expresses the nature.

With this background we can understand the deep significance of calling upon the name of the Lord. The name of Jesus expresses His nature as Savior. Nothing is so fitting to Jesus as saving us from our sins. When we name His name, we touch His saving life. Just to say "Jesus" brings with it the consciousness of His saving nature. His name represents His nature, character, function, history, and destiny. It is all concentrated in His name.

When we live under this revelation, whenever we speak the name "Jesus," the whole universe stands up at attention. Embodied in His name is His person, work, and position in the universe. At the name of Jesus every knee bows and every tongue confesses that Jesus Christ is Lord. So when we speak that name, we are touching the content of all that is in His person, work, and position. It is with this Biblical background that we gain a deeper appreciation of the significance of the name of the Lord.

*Changing a name meant changing a person's character, status, and destiny*

Another important matter related to the significance of names in the Bible is the changing of a person's name. To change a person's name meant to change his character, status, and destiny. For example, Abraham's original name was Abram (Gen. 11:26—17:5). But after the Lord appeared to him when he was ninety-nine years old and spoke to him of His covenant, Abram's name was changed (Gen. 17:1-5). Abram meant "father of elevation" or "exalted father." But because Abram's destiny under God's calling was to become "a father of many nations," God changed his name according to his new destiny. His new name "Abraham" more accurately expressed what God would do through him — "a father of many nations" or "a father of a multitude." Thus, the changing of a name represented something that happened in the character, status, and destiny of that person.

One of the most outstanding examples of a name change that reveals the change in the character of a person is the change of Jacob's name to Israel. Jacob meant "supplanter." The name Jacob expressed the exact feature of his fallen natural life: a person seeking to overthrow others by deception and trickery. From birth Jacob was trying to compete with and overreach his twin brother, Esau. While they were being born, he took hold of Esau's heel as they were coming out of their mother's womb (Gen. 25:24-26). Later, by trickery he took Esau's birthright and blessing (Gen. 25:27-34; 27:1-41). He was named Jacob because it perfectly expressed his "being on top of everything" nature. The name Jacob has stamped into it a supplanting nature. The name fits the nature, and the nature is expressed in the name.

Eventually, after many troubling experiences, Jacob's name was changed to Israel. Israel means "prince of God" or "God prevails." This name change reflected a change in Jacob's experience and destiny (Gen. 32:24-30). There was a change in Jacob's person, and the name "Israel" expressed that. Again, we see that in the Bible a name signifies character, status, and destiny. These examples are sufficient to show us the significance of naming in the Bible.

### The meaning of the name Jesus

We can summarize by saying that the name embodies the person. The name represents the person himself — his nature, character, status, function, destiny, and history. It is all concentrated in the name. So when we speak the name of Jesus, this is direct contact with His person and all that is in His person. He was begotten of the Holy Spirit, and the angel said to Joseph, "And you shall call His name JESUS, for He will save His people from their sins." The name Jesus is a contraction of two words. The first part of that name is *Hayah* or *Yahweh* or *Jehovah*, and as a verb it means "I am." It comes from the infinitive "to be," which is translated in the Old Testament as "I AM THAT I AM." Throughout the Old Testament, God revealed Himself in His names. And one of the chief revelations of Himself was in His name *Jehovah,* which means "I AM — I am present. I am existing. I am here. And I'll become everything to you." This is the name *Jehovah.* So when God revealed Himself in His name *Jehovah,* He was revealing His nature, His character, His existence, the kind of person He is, the way He is: "I AM. I am present. I am here." So in the first part of Jesus' name is *Jehovah,* I AM.

The second part of His name is "salvation." So what we have in the one name — Jesus — is "I AM salvation." To say "Jesus" is to announce a present-tense reality that He is on the scene, He is on the site, and He is here to save. To say "Jesus" is to say "I AM salvation. I am present." His person in His resurrected state as the Spirit is made available for us to so easily contact by simply uttering that name, Jesus. When we say "Jesus," we touch the Person. And the Person we touch is the I AM who is salvation: "I am saving you right now." We do not have a kind of relationship with the Lord that is remote. We do not have tech support by telephone. Jesus is on-site. Let me illustrate. At the office many things go wrong with our computers. There are so many things we do not understand, so many things we can't figure out. But we have on-site brothers who know all the workings of computers. And when they are on-site, "salvation" happens. In the same way, when we say "Jesus," He is on-site! He is here! It is Him! "I AM salvation."

# 2 ❱ The Revelation of God in His Names

*Calling upon the name of the Lord in the lowest dungeon*

Calling upon the name of the Lord is precious to desperate people. When you are desperate, you value calling on His name as Jeremiah does in Lamentations chapter 3. Here Jeremiah is mourning about the overwhelming problems he is under, and it seems that he just cannot get through them. He says to the Lord in verse 44, "You have covered Yourself with a cloud, that prayer should not pass through." Even prayer is not able to break through the problems. In verses 45-54 he depicts the severity of the situation: [45] "You have made us an offscouring and refuse in the midst of the peoples. [46] All our enemies have opened their mouths against us. [47] Fear and a snare have come upon us, desolation and destruction. [48] My eyes overflow with rivers of water for the destruction of the daughter of my people. [49] My eyes flow and do not cease, without interruption, [50] till the LORD from heaven looks down and sees. [51] My eyes bring suffering to my soul because of all the daughters of my city. [52] My enemies without cause hunted me down like a bird. [53] They silenced my life in the pit and threw stones at me. [54] The waters flowed over my head; I said, I am cut off!" When you reach the point of saying, "I am cut off!" you are at the bottom. You may have never reached that point, but Jeremiah in Lamentations 3 is at this lowest point. It is in this desperate hour that Jeremiah reacts in verses 55-57: [55] "I called on Your name, O LORD, from the lowest pit. [56] You have heard my voice: do not hide Your ear from my sighing, from my cry for help. [57] You drew near on the day I called on You, and said, Do not fear!"

When you call on Him out of the lowest pit, the Lord comes to you. He draws near. Notice that to call on His name (v. 55) is to call on Him (v. 57). His name *is* Him! When prayer did not work, and self's energy came to its end, calling upon the name of the Lord brought God in with His fear-dispelling speaking. What a wonderful reality that we can call on the name of Jesus. And when we call that name, we get His Person. For example, when I call out your name, immediately you respond to me. I get you yourself — I get your attention with all that you are. How marvelous that we can call Jesus' name and have Jesus, with His attention and all that He is. It is just by the mention of His name.

If the name of the Lord is the Lord Himself coming to us, we need to study the significance of the name of Jesus in the Scriptures. We need to see all the aspects of the precious name of Jesus. This will infuse us with faith and deepen our calling upon that name which is above every name.

## THE REVELATION OF GOD IN HIS NAMES

The significance of the name of the Lord has the entire Old Testament as a background. God chose to reveal by His names what kind of God He is in His nature, character, and work. His names tell us who He is, what He does, and what He will do. There are several names of God given to us in the Old Testament by which He reveals Himself. It is enlightening to see how God is revealed in His names.

### Elohim

The first name of God used in the Bible is *Elohim* (Gen. 1:1). This name is used well over two thousand times in the Old Testament, and is the most prominent name of God in the first chapters of the

Bible. When God is spoken of in His creation of the heavens and the earth, He is called *Elohim: Elohim* created, *Elohim* made, *Elohim* said. As *Elohim,* God unveils Himself in His creating power, by which He speaks something into being out of nothing. He is the God who spoke this universe into being because He is the almighty, creating God. So when God reveals Himself as *Elohim,* He is unveiling Himself as the kind of God who creates things out of nothing. He is the God of power to create and make the universe. Hallelujah! This is our God. How precious is His name *Elohim.*

## *El Shaddai*

Let us look at another name God used to communicate the kind of Person He is — *El Shaddai. El* means God, and *Shaddai* is from the Hebrew word *shad*, which means udder. The udder is that part of a cow which contains all the milk, that is, all the nourishment, all the supply. So this name means "the almighty, nourishing, satisfying, and supplying One." In Genesis 17:1 God said to Abraham, "I am *El Shaddai*" (ASV). That means "I am the God who will nourish you, supply you, and put everything into you that you will ever need." This is our God. How do we know God? He comes to us and tells us that His name is *El Shaddai*. He said this to Abraham when Abraham was ninety-nine years old and not able to have children. Thirteen years earlier he had tried to produce an heir through Hagar, his concubine; but God had rejected Ishmael as the heir (vv. 18-19). Now it seemed that all hope, all possibility, of having an heir was gone. Sarah, Abraham's wife, was ninety years old and passed the age of childbearing. And he himself was ninety-nine. So God had to show Himself. He appeared to Abraham and said, "I am *El Shaddai*. Walk before Me and be perfect." How? "I will be the udder to you. I will be that loving supply and nourishment. I will be everything to you to strengthen you." So God comes in His names, and His names tell us all about His Person.

## *Adonai*

Throughout the Old Testament God also reveals Himself as *Adonai*, which means Lord. He is the Lord. He is the Ruler. *Adonai* is the name that the Jews traditionally use to speak of God. Even to this day they feel strongly that the name *Jehovah*, or

*Yahweh,* is too sacred and too holy to utter. So when the Jews read the Bible today and come across the name *Jehovah,* they do not say *Jehovah;* they say *Adonai.* They will say *Lord,* but they will not say *Jehovah.* This is very significant, because *Jehovah* means Jesus. In John 8:24 Jesus says to the Jews, "Therefore I said to you that you will die in your sins; for unless you believe that I am, you will die in your sins." Then in verse 28 He says to them, "When you lift up the Son of Man, then you will know that I am, and that I do nothing from Myself, but as My Father has taught Me, I speak these things." And again in verse 58 He says to them, "Truly, truly, I say to you, before Abraham was, I AM." This means "Before Abraham came into being, I AM." Then the next verse tells us that they picked up stones to throw at Him. This is because He identified Himself as *Jehovah.*

## Jehovah and His suffixes

*Jehovah* means I AM. We may not have realized that the first part of the name Jesus means *Jehovah.* So the name Jesus includes this revelation — I AM. He wants us to know that when we call His name, He is what we need. At that moment, He is that. This is the revelation of the Person of *Jehovah.* And when we call, we get the Person of that name. And *Jehovah* means "I AM THAT I AM. I am the self-existing One. Just stay in contact with Me and I will be everything." So God reveals Himself in His name *Jehovah.*

As the Old Testament saints went through different kinds of experiences and contacted the Lord and touched Him and trusted Him, new names were added to *Jehovah. Jehovah-Yahweh*, the I AM, the self-existent, happening, becoming One, means "I am the One happening." To say "Jesus" means "Lord, You are the One happening right now." We may be in the middle of our reaction and our feelings and our distress. We cannot save ourself, and we say, "Jesus." That means "I AM the One that will happen in you, that will impart My life to you." This is the meaning of His name — I AM.

In Genesis 22 God tested Abraham by asking him to offer his son Isaac as a burnt offering to Him. As Abraham proceeded to take Isaac to the place of the burnt offering, Isaac asked his father, "Where is the lamb for a burnt offering?" And Abraham said, "My son, God will provide for Himself the lamb" (vv. 7-8). And God did provide. He told Abraham not to slay his son, but to kill the ram that was caught in the thicket nearby. So Abraham offered up the ram as a burnt offering to God. And it was at that place that the Lord's name was unveiled as *Jehovah-Jireh* — I AM the One who provides. That was an experience where Abraham was obeying God, not knowing what the next step would be. But as he was in contact with God, he was touching the I AM who provides on the spot, exactly when you need it and not before. This is our relationship with Him. To say "Jesus" is to touch the I AM who provides whatever you need.

Let us consider a practical example. Think about your finances. Think about your bills. Think about your debt. Think about your cogitations over how you are going to make ends meet. Think about all the anxiety that rushes into your heart and mind so that sometimes you cannot even sleep because you are so caught in the thicket of finances. Do you know that this is the perfect raw material to call "Jesus" and find Him as "I AM will provide"! He may be telling you to give to the church, but you are thinking, "How can I do it? I don't have enough. So I'll have to wait until next month." You are wondering how you can take care of all your needs. This is the time to call

"Jesus!" Give Him your firstfruits. Don't even think that you have a decision to make. Touch the One who became firstfruits to God in resurrection, the One who offered Himself in the freshness of His resurrection first to His Father. Then all our giving, all our handling of money, will tell the universe that what we have and what we possess does not belong to us. It is entrusted to us. We are only a steward.

It is only God's blessing that we have a roof over our head and that we have the job that we have, because He could take it in a second. Look at how people's lives change in just a short time. Look at the floods. Look at the earthquakes. Look at the tornadoes. People are existing with homes and happiness and cars, and within just a few hours everything is gone. God is our existence. God Himself is. So when the temptations come to us causing us to cogitate, to consider our financial situation and put the Lord aside, that is the time when you need the on-site *Jehovah*. Tell Him, "Lord, I need you on-site right now." And He will respond, "I AM salvation. I will save you from your money-loving heart that grips you. I will break the power of that. But you give." Let Him provide for you. Let Him prove Himself to you in this way. This is our God. This is the name of Jesus. It is *Jehovah,* meaning I AM.

In Exodus 15:26 the Lord revealed Himself as *Jehovah-Rapha*—I AM heals. At this time the Egyptians had all kinds of diseases, but the Lord covenanted with His people that He would bring none of those diseases of the Egyptians upon them. And then He "sealed" His covenant with the revelation of Himself as *Jehovah-Rapha:* I AM heals. "I am the LORD who heals you." This is the name of Jesus, and this is the power and the content of that name.

Exodus 17 is an account of the children of Israel being attacked by Amalek as they came out of Egypt. Amalek in typology signifies the flesh. It is a picture of the flesh. Moses stood on the top of a hill with the rod of God in his hand while Joshua and the children of Israel fought with Amalek. And verse 11 says, "And so it was, when Moses held up his hand, that Israel prevailed; and when he let down his hand, Amalek prevailed." So Aaron and Hur supported Moses' hands as he prayed and interceded during the battle between Israel and Amalek. This is like the battle between the flesh and the Spirit. And the battle was won as they kept Moses' hands up. This shows the necessity to be in contact with *Jehovah* all the time. In the midst of the battle, be in contact. While there is a struggle, *Jehovah* has to be held up. The prayer has to be going up. The calling has to go up. After Joshua's defeat of Amalek, the Lord said to Moses, "I will utterly blot out the remembrance of Amalek from under heaven" (v. 14). Then Moses built an altar and called its name *Jehovah-Nissi,* "The-Lord-Is-My-Banner," for he said, "Because the Lord has sworn: the Lord will have war with Amalek from generation to generation" (vv. 15-16). So the battle is the Lord's, and He is *Jehovah-Nissi,* "my banner, my victory." Let's tell it abroad — Jesus is Lord in the midst of the battle.

In Exodus 31:13 the Lord reveals Himself as *Jehovah-qadash* — I AM sanctifies. In commanding the children of Israel to keep His Sabbaths, He was revealing Himself as the One who makes holy, who sets apart. His name is revealed in His sanctifying work. His name expresses the nature, the function, the character, of His person. So here is *Jehovah-qadash* sanctifying His people to Himself.

In Jeremiah 23:6 and 33:16 the Lord connects salvation and safety with His name *Jehovah-Tsidkenu,* "THE LORD OUR RIGHTEOUSNESS." Your standing and my standing is not based on how we feel about ourselves. That is not our righteousness. We are never saved or safe in our own standing. Our standing is THE LORD OUR RIGHTEOUSNESS. So we can open our mouth. We can praise Him because *Jehovah,* I AM, is our righteousness.

In the book of Judges the Lord reveals Himself as *Jehovah-Shalom,* which means *Jehovah* is peace. When Gideon was afraid for his life because he had seen the Lord face to face, the Lord said to him, "Peace be with you; do not fear, you shall not die." So Gideon built an altar there to the Lord and called it *Jehovah-Shalom* (Judg. 6:23-24).

At the end of Ezekiel the Lord reveals Himself as *Jehovah-Shammah,* meaning "I AM is there." Ezekiel 48:35 says, "The name of the city from that day shall be:  THE LORD IS THERE."  The Lord Himself is there.  This is the way God reveals Himself in His names.  His names tell us about His nature, His person. The following is a list of what He is to His people as Jehovah, the I AM, the self-existing, becoming One:

1) *Jehovah-jireh*
I AM-provides (Gen. 22:8)
2) *Jehovah-rapha*
I AM-heals (Exo. 15:26)

3) *Jehovah-nissi*
I AM-my banner (Exo. 17:15-16)
4) *Jehovah-qadash*
I AM-sanctifies (Exo. 31:13)
5) *Jehovah-tsidkenu*
I AM-our righteousness (Jer. 23:6)
6) *Jehovah-shalom*
I AM-peace (Judg. 6:24)
7) *Jehovah-shammah*
I AM-there (Ezek. 48:35)

At every point, with every need, under every kind of circumstance, the Lord revealed Himself to His people as I AM WHO I AM. Just call *Jehovah* and fill in your suffix, and He will be I AM to you for your every need.

## *Experiencing God in His names*

In each of these passages the Lord's name was given after some kind of experience. God did not just give His people a list of His names and ask them to study them and be able to repeat them. It wasn't that way. They went through actual experiences where they touched the I AM in this way and in that way. His name kept coming out as there was an unveiling of the different aspects of His nature, of His provision, of who He was, of what He was to His people. In the New Testament these different aspects are called the unsearchable riches of Christ. So when we call the name Jesus, we can add on our suffix.

You may be having a difficult time as a wife. You can't be a "Bible wife." You are not that submissive. You can feel all that thunder beneath the surface of your being that wants to break out against your husband. You need to know that in the heat of your feelings of insubordination in your home, there is a name you can call — Jesus. *Jehovah* is the wife. "God, You are related to my husband. What a new world this is. It is as if someone opened the door. It is not just a natural relationship with him anymore. I have been transferred out of myself into the I AM who is the supply to know every move, facial expression, act of kindness, and ministry of life to this man." Then the Lord is *Jehovah-wife.* We could have a long list of suffixes. And in eternity I believe we will be at the dining table with Abraham, Isaac, and Jacob, feasting on all the suffixes of Jehovah. Praise the Lord! God reveals Himself in His names.

# 3 ▶ The Economy and Process of the Name

*The name inherited in eternity past*

With the Biblical background of the significance of names and of God revealing Himself in His names, we can now consider the economy and the process of the name of Jesus. The name of Jesus has a long process attached to it. It starts in eternity past, before creation. According to Proverbs 8:22-23 the Lord Jesus in His economy was established in eternity past: 22 "The LORD possessed me at the beginning of His way, *before* His works of old. 23 I have been established from everlasting, from the beginning, *before* there was ever an earth." Hebrews 1:2-4 also speaks about the Lord in relation to eternity past: 2 "[God] has in these last days spoken to us by His Son, whom He has appointed Heir of all things, through whom also He made the universe; 3 who being the brightness of His glory and the express image of His person, and upholding all things by the word of His power, when He had by Himself purged our sins, sat down at the right hand of the Majesty on high, 4 having become so much better than the

angels, as He has by inheritance obtained a more
excellent name than they." Christ was appointed
"Heir of all things," and as Heir He became the
means through which God made the universe. This
implies that the heirship of Christ was in eternity
past.

The Lord obtaining "a more excellent name"
than the angels indicates that the Lord's name in all
of its depths reaches back into eternity past, when the
entire angelic realm knew that the universe was to be
centered and focused in Christ. Verse 4 implies that
in eternity past the Lord inherited the name which is
above every name — the name of Jesus. At that time
all the angels and all the archangels had to behold the
fact that the Father designated His Son to be preemi-
nent, to be over everything. Colossians 1:16 says
that everything was created *in* Him, *through* Him,
and *unto* Him. This reveals that Christ was designated as the intrinsic reality of creation, as the means
and agent of creation, and as the goal of all creation.
The Father elevated His Son to be the Heir of all
things with a more excellent name than all the angels.

In those pre-Adamic ages, Lucifer, an archangel
and anointed cherub, was created by God as a beautiful creature and was appointed to lead the universe

in worship to Christ and to the Father (Ezek. 28:13-14). But iniquity was found in him and he became the devil, the one who rebelled against God (Ezek. 28:15; Isa. 14:13-14). In light of the heirship of Christ in the universe, we may well understand *why* Lucifer wanted to be like the Most High. It was no doubt related to the Father lifting up His Son, Jesus Christ, by appointing Him Heir of all things and giving Him a name above every name. Christ was designated to be the centrality of the whole universe. Lucifer beheld all this heavenly activity with Christ as the center. He watched it all, he heard it all, and he knew it all. Then in his heart he was lifted up and he rebelled against God's order of things and became the devil. Thus, his fall as Satan was related to the One who inherited the most excellent name.

The scene in eternity past was around Jesus Christ as the centrality and supremacy of the whole universe, with the name that Satan rebelled against — the name that is more excellent than all the angels. That is why today when we say "Jesus," included in that name is what He inherited in eternity past, what distinguished Him as being better than all the angels, including that fallen angel. So when we say "Jesus," we are agreeing and corresponding with what the heavens said in eternity past concerning this Person. The name of Jesus always causes Satan to fall because that name is above every name.

Today the enemy may try to invade your thought-life and fill up your emotion with bitterness, hate, hardness, and all that demonic activity in the realm of the soul. If you wonder what to do with a mind and emotion that are in confusion and frustration, there is an answer. Speak the name Jesus. Call the name Jesus. That name has been inherited from eternity past, and every demon knows that name (Acts 19:15). Satan knows that name, and he doesn't want you to speak it. He doesn't want you to open your mouth. But what should we do? We have the name that is above every name. At the name of Jesus, Satan has to bow. Every knee must bow at the name of Jesus. He has inherited a more excellent name in this universe. This inheritance came out of eternity past. The name of Jesus goes back to God's original thought for the universe. The economy and process of the name of Jesus is linked with all God's eternal counsels and plans coming out of eternity past. When we call that precious name, Jesus, we get linked to that same eternal dimension.

*Incarnation is embodied in the name*

That name has a history. Everything that Jesus has experienced, everything He has passed through, is now concentrated and embodied in the name. That means that everything that is in that Person is concentrated and embodied in His name. Eternity past is in that name. His incarnation is in that name. His human life is in that name — his living for 331/2 years, from one incident to another, from suffering, to facing sin, to struggling against sin, to winning every battle over every sin attack. Hebrews 12:4 says that He struggled against sin, and He overcame every time. He became in the likeness of this fallen nature, and He concluded this Adamic race victoriously.

This race was concluded victoriously because Jesus came "in the likeness of the flesh of sin and concerning sin," and He condemned sin in the flesh both by His life and by His death (Rom. 8:3). So He is called the last Adam. He brought the whole human race to its proper conclusion: "I am the last one of the race." This means there are no other conclusions. He did it. And He became a life-giving Spirit. This is His Person now. So God became a man, and that man lived for 331/2 years. And that manhood was brought into God. It was saturated with God, so that now He is the God-Man in resurrection. He is the last Adam, the life-giving Spirit.

That last-Adam life properly concluded the race and fulfilled God's original intention from Genesis 1 — to have man in His image. And now, who is His image? Christ is His image. He is the image of the invisible God. And He is the image in humanity: As a man, He won all the battles with sin, with the flesh, with the world, and with the devil; and He brought humanity fully into God. So when we say "Jesus," He is saying, "I AM the salvation in your humanity, the kind of salvation to transform you and to bring your living — to bring your home, to bring your clothing, to bring your talking, to bring your habits — into God." This is what happens in the name of Jesus. We touch what is in that name: eternity past, incarnation, human living, the cross — what He did there, what He accomplished there — and resurrection.

*The human living of Christ is embodied in the name*

The first step in the process of the name of Jesus began in eternity past. The next step in the process of that name was the incarnation. At the time of the incarnation an angel of the Lord said to Joseph, "You shall call His name JESUS, for He will save His people from their sins" (Matt. 1:21). So the name of Jesus includes what transpired in the incarnation — the Word, God Himself, became flesh (John 1:14).

The next step in the process of the name of Jesus was His human living. Man was fallen. Man was flesh. There was no hope for man. There was no way man could save himself. Four thousand years of history, from Genesis to the time that the Lord came into the world, proved one thing — there is no hope for the flesh. No one could make it. Corruptible flesh is fallen. But then in the fullness of time, "God sent forth His Son, born of a woman" (Gal. 4:4).

The Son of God became a man. He was just like you and me. He had skin. He had bones. He had blood. He was a human being. And He lived a human life, incarnated for those 33 1/2 years. He experienced emotions. He experienced temptation. He experienced the attacks of the enemy. He went through human life in every dimension. He went through all the battles, struggling against sin (Heb. 12:3-4), and He came off perfect and victorious (Heb. 7:26). He brought humanity into what God wanted humanity to be from the beginning — in His image (Gen. 1:26-28; cf. Col. 1:15).

Christ brought God into man, and He brought man into God. He brought humanity into God — this is what transpired in His human living. He was the last Adam and the second Man (1 Cor. 15:45, 47). As the last Adam, He brought the old race to its proper conclusion. He was the *last* of Adam's race. The race had become fallen and He came "in the likeness of the flesh of sin and concerning sin," and judged and condemned sin in the flesh (Rom. 8:3).

Christ condemned sin in the flesh both by His life and by His death. He took human nature and brought it into God without sin! He condemned sin in the flesh as He lived a life in the flesh apart from sin. Sin did not win a single victory in His 331/2 years. It was thoroughly condemned by His spotless, sinless life. And at the cross He concluded His last-Adam life. Then wonder of wonders — He brought His last-Adam life and victory into resurrection to become a life-giving Spirit. Now He can come into us and impart *that* life to us.

Christ as the last Adam who became a life-giving Spirit is now in our spirit. And He is giving His life away to all who call upon His name. Indeed, He is rich unto all who call upon Him (Rom. 10:12-13). When we call "Jesus," we are taking Him as our person with His emotions, His mind, His attitudes, His will, and His victory. Calling His name makes Him life-giving to our inner being. This is the deep significance of calling upon the name of the Lord. It is a direct participation in the process of His incarnation and human living made available in the Spirit. It is all in that precious name!

### Crucifixion is embodied in the name

When you say "Jesus," you are touching His Person. And when you touch His Person, you are touching the intrinsic history of that Person. This includes not only incarnation and human living, but also what took place on the cross — what happened at Calvary. Calvary is where the old creation was terminated. It is where sins were dealt with, and the sin nature itself was dealt with. Jesus did it all. And the Father accepted that Sacrifice. It is so finished, it is so perfect, that the Lord has the boldness to say what He said in John 16:26: "In that day you will ask in My name, and I do not say to you that I will ask the Father concerning you." Now, we would say, "But

Lord, don't leave me out. I need someone to talk to the Father about me." In this verse there are two Greek words for "ask." The first word is at the beginning of the verse and is what we normally translate as "ask." But the second Greek word is different. When the Lord says, "I do not say to you that I will *ask* the Father concerning you," He uses the word for beseeching and begging: "I am not going to beseech and beg the Father concerning you." But please do not misunderstand. He is just saying, "I am not a Catholic saint who is going to pray for you."

I remember that when I was growing up as a Catholic, they used to tell me, "Jesus is too busy, so you need Mary, you need Saint Christopher, you need Saint Joseph. Talk to Saint Joseph, talk to Christopher, and they will take all your needs to Jesus, because Jesus is too busy to talk to you." So we needed someone to talk to someone else for us. But Jesus says, "I do not say to you that I will beg the Father concerning you. In that day, just ask in My name, because My name is My Person." This means that your whole inner attitude at any moment, at any time, under any situation, can be without one hesitation — we always have direct access to the Father.

Jesus is saying, "My work and My blood is so perfect and so finished and so eternal that it is standing there in the heavens. Five bleeding wounds I bear, received on Calvary. They pour effectual prayers. They strongly speak for you. So I do not have to go through any religious method to get to My Father. I am not going to beg My Father about you, because you are okay. I put Me in you. You have My name. And when you have My name, you have Me. And My work is finished, and My Father is satisfied. So I am not begging for anything. So you quit begging and start commanding — Father, Father! — because it is Me in you."

### *The name and His death,*
### *burial, resurrection, and exaltation*

The One who inherited a more excellent name than the angels (Heb. 1:4) is the same One who through death destroyed "him who had the power of death, that is, the devil" (Heb. 2:14). The name of Jesus has been processed through the death of a cross, where sin, Satan, the flesh, the world, and the entire old creation were terminated and defeated (Phil. 2:8). And then He took the name through His burial. He was buried, but His soul could not be kept in Hades (Acts 2:27-32). It did not belong there. It *passed through* death (Rev. 1:18). And then the name came forth in resurrection, and God highly exalted Him and gave Him the name which is above every name — the name of Jesus!

## The Lord's person and work concentrated in His name

The Lord's person and work is now concentrated in His name. This is the ultimate point to which we come. All of the Lord's person — all of what He is, everything that He has done, all of His finished work — is now concentrated in the name Jesus. He is such an unsearchably rich Christ. Calling Jesus' name is like taking a pill that has an all-inclusive dose of vitamins and minerals. It has Vitamin A, B-complex, C, E, and so forth. All the proper things that are necessary for our body are concentrated in that one pill. If we just take that pill, we get it all. In the same way, the name Jesus is the concentration of all His person and all His work.

First Corinthians 6:11 says that we were washed, we were sanctified, and we were justified "in the name of the Lord Jesus Christ and in the Spirit of our God." So washing was applied to us. Sanctification was applied to us. Justification was applied to us. All of what the Lord did for us is applied to us in a concentrated way in the name of the Lord Jesus. It is this name which evokes the Spirit of our God to bring our whole being into the reality of all that is in the name.

### The name being the link between Christ's person in the flesh and Christ's person as the Spirit

In John 14—16 there is a seamless link between Christ's person in the flesh and His person in the Spirit. It is a bridge showing us how Christ in the flesh continues as Christ as the Spirit. And the bridge is His name. He kept saying to the disciples, "Don't be troubled. I know you are going to suffer a little bit, and everyone will be scattered — all this is going to happen. And you are all distressed about My going away." This is the conversation in John 14, 15, and 16. He was with them in the flesh, and now they were having all kinds of interaction between them because they were disturbed about His leaving. He was right there in the flesh, but He kept interjecting all these words: "I am going to send the Spirit. And when He comes, I am coming. He is abiding with you, and shall be in you." Then He says, "I am coming to you." This means "I am doing it. I am going to be there." And yet they could hardly understand it. He was saying, "The bridge between My being with you in the flesh and My being with you in the Spirit is My name. I am giving you My name. You will start asking in My name. And you will be coming to the Father in My name. That means in My Person. My Person is now linked to My name. Before, you handled Me in the flesh. Now when I become the Spirit, the way you will handle Me is by My name. My name is My Person. My name is the link between Me and the Spirit. So I will be in you and you will know that I am in the Father, and the Father is in Me, and you are in Me. You are going to know this wonderful life. It is all in My name."

### *The way to touch the riches of the Lord's person and finished work*

Calling upon the name of Jesus is the way to touch the riches of the Lord's person and finished work. Oh, brothers and sisters, how precious it is to hear these wonderful things about the name of Jesus. This name includes His history and His process. And knowing His name also means knowing His person. To know the name is to know the person. And to call His name is to touch His person. So our Christian life and all that God is accomplishing in us is reduced to our deeply touching Jesus by calling upon His name.

*All that is in the name of Jesus!*

Now consider the process of the name in the diagram below:

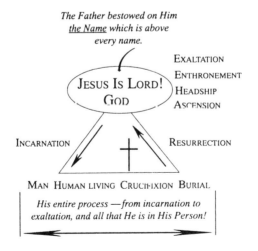

*The Father bestowed on Him the Name which is above every name.*

JESUS IS LORD!
GOD

EXALTATION
ENTHRONEMENT
HEADSHIP
ASCENSION

INCARNATION

RESURRECTION

MAN HUMAN LIVING CRUCIFIXION BURIAL

*His entire process —from incarnation to exaltation, and all that He is in His Person!*

Consider all that is in the name of Jesus. He was God. He became a man. He lived a human life. He was crucified, buried, and resurrected. Then He ascended, and being highly exalted, He was given the name which is above every name. As God He had that name in eternity past. But then He became a man and lived for 331/2 years and actually defeated the devil every inch of the way. Then He ascended through the atmosphere far above all, and one day in this universe there was a grand bestowal by the Father. Philippians 2:9 says that God "bestowed on Him the name which is above every name." Jesus had made it through — He passed through the heavens. Now as our High Priest, He can sympathize with us moment by moment because He was a man (Heb. 4:14-16). He passed through every experience, and now He is the Lord. He is the Lord in this universe.

Look at the name of Jesus. Look at the process the name has gone through. So when we need crucifixion to this flesh, we say "Jesus." In that name is the putting to death: "Flesh, you are not going to whimper here. You are not going to suffer here. You are not going to hang on and keep yourself alive for the last few minutes of your existence." Just "Jesus," and at that name the cross is applied. There is termination. You interrupt your emotions. You interrupt that sulking. You interrupt that thing that wants to keep limping. Jesus! There is crucifixion in that name.

Sometimes you feel dead. You feel like there is no life. But there is resurrection in that name. When you say "Jesus," you come out of the grave. That name has resurrection in it. It is resurrection. And now that name has been given to the church. It is Jesus who is now Lord and Christ. And we are responding by bowing our knee and confessing with our mouth, "Lord Jesus." And there is no other name under heaven given among men by which we must be saved (Acts 4:12).

## *Taking Christ as your person through His name*

Ultimately we come to this experiential point — taking Christ as our person through His name. Brothers and sisters, Christ is our person. He is our new person. He is the One in our spirit who is saying, "I AM. I am present, on-site salvation. I am going to do it all." Whatever we see in ourselves, He takes care of it all. He is our person. And the way we enjoy

Him and take Him as our person in our daily life is by His name, because His name is the appointed means for us to have a handle, to have a practical grip, to experience Christ in the middle of everything. This is how you take Him as your person.

You are feeling depressed, you are feeling hopeless about yourself. Of course! These feelings are programmed into the flesh. They are six thousand years old. That is fallen man — hopeless, depressed. Now, at that moment you need to take Christ as your person and not you as your person. How do you take Him in the middle of those feelings? You just open your mouth and say "Jesus." To say "Jesus" is to get His Person with the "I AMness" in Him. By speaking His name to your thoughts, to your feelings, to the atmosphere, to anything negative, you make a transfer and you actually live by Christ as your person.

Not only do I experience Him in the negative things, but even positively I do not want to just coast as a human being in my own goodness. I want Jesus to fill my life, so I am pouring out that name. That means He is my person. In 2 Corinthians 2:10 Paul does not rely on his own ability to forgive, but instead takes Christ as his person. He says to the believers,

"But whom you forgive anything, I also forgive; for also what I have forgiven, if I have forgiven anything, it is for your sake *in the person of Christ."* In this situation a young man had committed incest and did not repent. While he was in that state, the church had to put him out. So everyone in the church knew about this young man. He had committed a kind of fornication that was worse than what was in the Gentile world — having immorality with his stepmother. So family and others were involved. Can you imagine the kind of feelings, hurts, and bitternesses that would be there?

But eventually this young man was handed over to the enemy. It was as if God said, "We will let the enemy do something over him to see if he will have a change of heart." And whatever Satan was allowed to do, it brought the young man to repentance. He was swallowed up with sorrow. Then Paul exhorted the believers, "Go and confirm your love to him. Forgive him. Now is the right time. Go to him now." Probably some thought, "Paul, how could we forgive? You don't know the situation. Our relatives were involved. This was immorality within the family. He should be ostracized forever. How can we forgive?" But Paul says, "Forgive." Actually the

Greek word is the verbal form of "grace." Grace him. This means he doesn't deserve it — no one deserves it — but grace him. Then Paul says, "I forgive. And if I forgive anything, I forgive it in the Person of Christ. I am not waiting for a feeling of forgiveness. I have forgiveness Himself living in me. He is my person. And I can call His name, Jesus, and transfer out of that hurt, hardness, and bitterness into another Person."

Oh, saints, we need to take Him as our person. This is not just a preaching. We have the name, and that name is Jesus. Oh, what a name! His Person is in His name. When you call "Jesus," from this moment on it will be a new world to you. Faith comes by hearing, and hearing by the Word of God. This is why we say "Jesus" — because we call and get the Person of that name!

# 4 ▶ Experiencing the Lord in His Name

ALL THAT IS IN THE NAME OF JESUS

*The Lord's person and work*
*are concentrated in His name*

Jesus! He is all in that wonderful name. Not only is the name all, but all of Jesus is in that name. Everything is in His precious name. We have to see that the concentration of all that the Lord is and all that He has accomplished is in His name. So regardless of what our need is, our need is Christ! Our need is Christ in what He is, and our need is Christ in what He has done — all this is to be applied to us.

Our need is Christ in every dimension. And it is marvelous to realize that all He is and all He has attained is now concentrated in the name Jesus. So when we say that name we drink Him, we partake of Him. He is available by that name and in that name. The Lord has made it so simple. He has put it right on the platter so that we can just enjoy and partake in a very simple way without complication, without having to do anything but breathe the name of Jesus.  We can just open our mouth in the middle of whatever or in the middle of nothing, and there is pure enjoyment of this Person.  In whatever we are passing through, we can speak the name of Jesus and know that in that name is Himself.  He has concentrated Himself in His name.

In 1 Corinthians 6:10 Paul speaks of those who will not inherit the kingdom of God.  Then in verse 11 he says to the believers, "And these things were some of you; but you were washed, but you were sanctified, but you were justified *in the name* of the Lord Jesus Christ and in the Spirit of our God."  So it is the name that qualifies us to inherit the kingdom.  In the name we were washed.  The washing is obviously based upon the precious blood of the Lamb, meaning that all He accomplished on Calvary is now being applied to us.  "You were washed" means that the benefits of that precious blood and of that finished work are now in the name of the Lord Jesus.  "You were sanctified and you were justified" refers to all that He accomplished for us in His finished work.  Everything that He passed through is now concentrated in the name of the Lord Jesus and in the Spirit of our God.  The name concentrates all the benefits and all the good of what

He has passed through, and the name releases the Spirit and operates the divine resurrection life into our being and through our being.

*Our vision when we call upon the name of the Lord*

We have to see how precious the name of Jesus is so that we will have vision when we call on that name. What is in our spiritual vision is crucial when we call upon the name of the Lord. It is as Paul says, "How then shall they call upon Him in whom they have not believed? And how shall they believe in Him of whom they have not heard? And how shall they hear without one who proclaims Him?" (Rom. 10:14). Paul is saying that there is some speaking, and the speaking is about Christ.

Then in verse 17 he says, "Faith comes out of hearing, and hearing through the word of Christ" — the word all about Christ. Just tell me about Jesus, and faith comes out of hearing. So here comes faith. Faith is being given to me as a gift. I'm sitting here, and in a sense I'm passive. I haven't done anything. I haven't rectified myseif. I haven't changed my life. I've come just the way I am, and I'm just here and I hear. I hear the word about Christ. And as the

word about Christ is being spoken or sung or testified or read — as the word about Christ is coming
— there is something in my heart. There is something that has enlarged me to just believe into this
One that I am hearing about. So what is happening
is that as I am hearing there is something generated
within my heart, and that something is called faith.

And then Paul says that out of the believing, out
of that faith operating, issues the calling: "How then
shall they call upon Him in whom they have not
believed? And how shall they believe in whom they
have not heard?" This indicates that there is a precious hearing, and out of this hearing there is an
enlargement of our heart into this believing. So when
we call "Jesus," it is because we have been infused
with the revelation of what He is and what He has
accomplished. The revelation has come by hearing;
it has come by the vision imparted to us through the
Word. As the Word is infused into us, it imparts this
vision. Then when we call "Jesus," we are partaking of all that He is and all that He has accomplished.
For example, at this moment in our calling we may
be partaking of His resurrection life. At another
moment it may be His crucifying life. And at still

another moment we may be partaking of the very attitudes of Jesus and the love of Jesus that is infused into our being as we call.

Everything is concentrated in the precious name of Jesus. All the Christian books you have ever read, all the instruction about knowing your identification with Christ — knowing that your old man has been crucified, knowing that you have been crucified to the world and the world to you, knowing that the enemy has been defeated and that we have all been raised up together and made to sit together with Christ in the heavenly places — everything that you know by knowledge in your mind is concentrated now in the reality that is in the name of Jesus. So now when we speak that name we get the good of that life. At a particular moment I need the putting to death of Jesus to something in my being. The crucifying life is in that name. When I am speaking that name, no one else may know it but I am drawing upon the putting to death of Jesus, putting to death this inordinate thought-life that wants to run wild and take its own thoughts and be independent from God. So when I am saying "Jesus," I am saying the name that has the crucifying in it.

*The name of Jesus is the continuation of Jesus*

Not only is everything concentrated in His name, but everything that He is continues in His name. The continuation of Jesus Christ, who is the same yesterday, today, and forever, is in His name. The name is the continuation of Jesus. We see this in the book of Acts. Luke begins the book of Acts by saying, "The former account [the Gospel of Luke] I have made, O Theophilus, concerning all the things that Jesus *began* both to do and to teach" (1:1). So Acts is a continuation of Luke's Gospel. The word "began" in this verse implies that now in the book of Acts Jesus is continuing. And how does He continue? In His name. It seems that all that is there in the chapters of Acts — all that the believers did — was based on the name of Jesus. They were doing things *in the name*. They were being commanded not to speak anymore *in that name* (4:17-18; 5:28, 40). And what they were being persecuted for was *the name*. So what dominates the scene in the book of Acts is that name.

In chapter 3 the man who was lame from birth was healed through faith in Jesus' name. Peter boldly declared to the religious leaders, "By the name of

Jesus Christ . . . by Him this man stands here before you whole" (4:10). Even on the day of Pentecost when Peter was preaching the gospel, eventually it consummated in that pinnacle, "Whoever calls on the name of the LORD shall be saved" (2:21). So what we see is the continuation of the Lord Jesus in the book of Acts by the name. The disciples were all identified as those who called on the name of the Lord. Before the Lord captured Saul of Tarsus and defeated him, he was binding all those who were calling upon the name (9:14).

By all these passages we can see that the continuation of Jesus is in the name. How wonderful! And it is in that name that the whole covenant of grace, the whole economy of grace that we are now under in this new dispensation, is preserved in our experience. John 1:17 says, "The law was given through Moses; grace and truth came through Jesus Christ." So the Lord's economy is an economy of grace, which means it is an economy of supply after supply after supply. To begin with, it is receiving Him as a free gift. And then it is continuing to receive Him as His grace is being dispensed into us day after day, day after day, until one day we will sing, "When we've been there ten thousand years, bright shining as the sun, we've no less days to sing God's praise than when we first begun." Hallelujah! There is amazing grace in His name.

*The name of Jesus and putting
ourselves in a receiving position*

All grace — this economy of grace — is preserved in our experience by His name. How? When you say "Jesus," you automatically put yourself in a receiving position. You are calling upon the name and you are drawing from His Person. You are expecting out of Him and being identified with Him rather than being under the stress and strain of your own energy and your own striving and your own rearrangement of your life — replacing your bad thoughts with good thoughts and making resolutions and arguing with your thought-life that you will be better next time. Calling saves us from all this.

But when you delay calling on Jesus, you remove yourself from the realm of grace. You spend needless time — moments and even hours — floating in that land where there is no hope. That is the wilderness. You wander and wander in the soul, and you leave the economy of grace and get into another

economy — the economy of the flesh; and it is
works, it is exhaustion.  But when you say "Jesus,"
you stay in the economy of grace.  When you are
about to react toward your husband, when you have
those feelings toward your husband, you need the
economy of grace right at that moment.  You feel
bad for those reactions.  As a sister in the Lord you
know you shouldn't react in that kind of way.  What
are you going to do with yourself?  You have to cast
yourself, throw yourself, upon Him.  And the way
you can keep yourself in the grace is just by whispering "Jesus," just "Jesus." By that you are drinking of another life, another source, another feeling,
another reaction.  Hallelujah!  It preserves us in this
wonderful economy of grace.  So everything is in
this precious name.  The continuation of Christ and
the concentration of His Person is in His name.

### The relationship between
### the Lord as the Spirit and His name

In John chapter 14 we see the relationship between the Lord as the Spirit and His name.  In verses
16-18 the Lord says, [16] "And I will ask the Father,
and He will give you another Comforter, that He

may be with you forever, [17] even the Spirit of reality, whom the world cannot receive, because it does not behold Him or know Him; but you know Him, because He abides with you and shall be in you. [18] I will not leave you as orphans; I am coming to you." Here the Lord is talking about the Spirit coming, and in the next phrase He says, "I am coming." So we know it is the Lord Himself who comes to us. Sometimes we say He comes *through* the Spirit, but more directly we can say He comes *as* the Spirit. When He says that the Spirit is coming and that the Spirit will be in you, He does not give all kinds of explanations. He just adds, "I will not leave you as orphans; I am coming to you." This means the coming of the Spirit is the coming of Jesus.

Here we see the divine economy of the Lord, with Him being so intimate to us and so close to us. He was telling the disciples, "Don't be bothered. Don't be troubled that I'm going away. If I'm going away I'm coming back again, and I'm coming back in the Spirit, even as the Spirit. And My relationship with you will be more intimate than it has ever been before because in that day you will know that I am in My Father and you in Me and I in you. You are going to know this because I will be in you and

I will bring you right into Our relationship. I'm going to let you actually participate in My relationship with the Father. I will put Our relationship right into your being. When the Spirit comes, He is your portion." So the Spirit and the Lord Himself are just together, are just one, in John 14.

### The sending of the Spirit and the Lord's name

Then in verse 26 the Lord says, "But the Comforter, the Holy Spirit, whom the Father will send in My name, He will teach you all things and remind you of all the things which I have said to you." When the Lord says that the Father will send the Spirit "in My name," it means that when we call His name, "Jesus," we activate the reality of the life-giving Person who is the Spirit today, the resurrected Jesus with all that He is (2 Cor. 3:17-18). We activate that Person by His name. So it is awesome to speak the name of Jesus. It activates the reality of the Spirit. That is why Paul puts the name and the Spirit together in 1 Corinthians 6:11. He says that we were washed, sanctified, and justified "in the name of the Lord Jesus Christ and in the Spirit of our God." How precious is this word.

### Life in His name

In John 20:31 we have a summary of John's whole Gospel: "But these have been written that you may believe that Jesus is the Christ, the Son of God, and that believing, you may have *life in His name.*" Jesus is the life-giver. He gives life, and He gives it in His name. John writes this whole Gospel with a purpose — that we would believe. This believing is into the precious name of Jesus, and in this name and by this name we have life.

So we can see the intimacy between His name and the life-giving Spirit, the giving of the life, the actual dispensing of the life. I need the life in my being. I need to be a different person. He gives life in His name. Brothers and sisters, all these verses, all the Word of God, should just infuse us to sanctify our lips by speaking that name "Jesus" with our heart, with our understanding, with vision, with our whole being. We are partakers and participators in the very life and nature of God by the name of Jesus.

### *The name of Jesus and being in the Holy Spirit*

In 1 Corinthians 12:3 Paul says, "No one can

say, Jesus is Lord! except in the Holy Spirit." Or it can be translated, "No one can say, Lord Jesus! except in the Holy Spirit." And in verse 13 Paul says, "For also in one Spirit we were all baptized into one body, whether Jews or Greeks, whether slaves or free, and were all given to drink one Spirit." This drinking of the one Spirit together as one Body is available to every saint. No one is left out. In these two verses why does Paul stress that the Spirit is available to every saint? Here in chapter 12 Paul is dealing with the operation of the gifts in the church meetings. It may have been that some were feeling certain ways about the gifts. Maybe some felt excluded from the Spirit if they did not have a more demonstrative kind of gift, whether it be speaking in tongues or the interpretation of tongues or the gift of prophecy or healing. Maybe some were comparing themselves with others and thinking, "Well, I don't have that operation of the Spirit passing through me." Maybe they felt a little bit excluded in the one Body. But it is so precious the way Paul begins this chapter. He just says, "No one can say, Lord Jesus! except in the Holy Spirit." That means every saint is a participator in the drink of the Spirit by just saying that name. This shows us how intimate the name is with the participation in the Holy Spirit.

## The Lord's doings and His name

In John 14:13-14 the Lord says, [13] "And whatever you ask in My name, that I will do, that the Father may be glorified in the Son. [14] If you ask Me anything in My name, I will do it." Do you see the connection? "My name" — "I will do it!" The Lord's name releases the Lord's doing. If you stay in yourself — looking at your feelings, analyzing your insides — nothing happens and you just go under the pile even more. But just as you are, caught in the middle of yourself, use your mouth with that name Jesus. You say "Jesus," and He says, "I will do it."

We are not the Savior. He is the Savior. We try to save ourselves, we try to fix ourselves up. But, brothers and sisters, He is the fixer-upper. And He is the fixer-upper by our calling upon the name of the Lord. Otherwise we are the fixer-upper: "Give *me* the credit. Give *me* the glory. Pat *me* on the back." But if I drop myself, humble myself, become weak, dependent, just a caller — "Jesus" — I get filled up. Then all the glory is to the Father, all the glory is to Him. The Lord is the doer of it all by His name. How precious is this name. So we can see the relationship between the Lord Himself as the Spirit, as the life-giver, as the doer, and this precious name.

# 5 ❭ Understanding Calling
# Upon the Name of the Lord

## THE MEANING OF THE WORD "CALLING" IN THE BIBLE

### The Hebrew word for call

Throughout the entire Old Testament, whenever calling upon the name of the Lord is mentioned, the Hebrew word *qara* is typically used. The dictionaries tell us that *qara* means to call, cry, or even utter a loud sound. In Isaiah 36:13 *qara* is translated "cried out with a loud voice." It means to call unto someone. And in Psalm 57:2 we see another usage of the word *qara:* to cry out to God. The psalmist says, "I will cry out to God Most High, to God who performs all things for me." Also in Psalm 147:9, a very simple verse, *qara* is used: "He gives to the beast its food, and to the young ravens that *cry*." These ravens are crying and the Lord gives them food. Here *qara* is translated "cry."

This same Hebrew word *qara* is used for call in Genesis 4:26: "Then men began to *call* on the name of the LORD." When they were weak, when they were at the point of no return in themselves, they began to call. So the same word that is used for the cry of a raven in one verse is used here for calling on the name of the Lord. It is definitely a calling that is out loud and a crying that goes to Him. With prayer you can be silent like Hannah, just moving your lips (1 Sam. 1:10-13). But it is impossible to call silently. Both the Hebrew and Greek words for calling mean to call out, to speak out that name, even to cry out, and sometimes with a loud voice. At other times it is just "Jesus" — maybe not loud, but you are calling. It is a calling upon the Person. This is the meaning of the Hebrew word *qara.*

## *The Greek word for calling upon*

The Greek word for call, *epikaleo,* means to invite and summon someone. It means to call to, to call upon, to appeal to, to call out, to cry out upon. And sometimes it means to surname or designate someone. These are the different definitions given in all the dictionaries for *epikaleo.* The word itself is a compound word. The first part of the word is the preposition *epi,* which means "upon." And this is prefixed to the root word *kaleo,* which is the word "call."

The word *kaleo* stands alone many times in the New Testament. For example, it is used in Romans 8:30: "And those whom He predestined, these He also called." This is *kaleo*. That means the Lord called us one day. This refers to His coming to us so that we would be saved. He called us through some means. But the word for calling is *epikaleo*. We add the *epi* prefix to the root word *kaleo* to emphasize the object called upon. The Greek preposition *epi* puts an intensive into the word "calling." It is not just calling in any direction. It is calling upon a specific object. And when it is used for calling upon the name of the Lord, it is a call that focuses and calibrates our whole being upon this Person. The very word *epikaleo* shows us that we gird up our loins, everything that is loose in us, and we call "Jesus." He becomes front and center: Attention! Everything stop. "Jesus." We are calling upon this Person. We are calling this Person in reality. This is the significance of the word "call."

*The middle voice and taking the initiative to call*

When related to calling on the name of the Lord, the Greek verb *epikaleo* is always used in the middle voice in the New Testament. In Greek *the active voice* stresses the subject as the doer of the action. *The middle voice* not only stresses the subject as performing the action but also as being involved in or participating in the result of the action. And *the passive voice* stresses the subject being acted upon. All the Greek grammarians tell you that it is impossible to accurately reproduce the thought of the middle voice with our English language. This is true of any language — there are certain unique inflections and idioms that cannot be reproduced or exactly translated into another language. You have to feel it. There is emotion in it. We all know in languages it is this way.

In Greek there is something unique whenever the middle voice is used. It means the subject is involved in the action of the verb, even participating in the action. This means that as the subject we are not passive. Neither is calling on the Lord stressing the action of calling as an end in itself. It is stressing our taking the initiative with our spirit and our mouth to call upon the name of the Lord. The emphasis is always upon our taking the initiative. We are involved in this action, and we participate in the result.

Again, wherever the word *epikaleo* is used for calling on the name of the Lord, it is exclusively in the middle voice. This indicates that it is not something you will be forced to do from without. It is not that you are passive and are acted upon. It means that you yourself and I myself open our mouth and we are involved in calling upon that name. So take the step. Take the initiative. If you have never done it, it may seem like jumping off the edge of a diving board for the first time. When I was a young boy, maybe 9 or 10 years old, I remember getting up on a 10-foot-high diving board and looking down for the first time. Oh, it looked scary to me. But eventually I had to jump off. Right? In the same way, you may feel like you are not sure if calling on the Lord will work for you. You say, "You don't know my condition." But I say, tell the self to be quiet. And you just call "Jesus." The self will talk incessantly. It will discourage. It is never ready. It is always waiting. It is always getting itself together. It is always doing something. So just cut through and call upon that name — "Jesus, Jesus." And then He is activated right within your being. So we can see the significance of the middle voice.

Here is a list of some of the verses that use the middle voice in the present, aorist, and future tenses:

*Present middle:* Acts 7:59; 9:14, 21; Rom. 10:12; 1 Cor. 1:2; 2 Tim. 2:22; 1 Pet. 1:17

*Aorist middle:* Acts 2:21; 22:16; Rom. 10:13

*Future middle:* Rom. 10:14

## The Greek word for crying

Another Greek word used for calling out upon the Lord is *krazo*. This word is even stronger than *epikaleo* in terms of the intensity of crying out. It means to cry, to cry out, to cry aloud, to speak with a loud voice. *Vine's Expository Dictionary* especially defines *krazo* as shrieking like a raven. This is the significance of this word.

Let us look at some examples of the use of *krazo* in the New Testament. It is used in Galatians 4:6: "And because you are sons, God has sent forth the Spirit of His Son into our hearts, *crying,* Abba, Father!" *Krazo* is also the word used when the Lord Jesus was crying out on the cross. Matthew 27:50 says, "And Jesus *cried out* again with a loud voice and yielded up His spirit." So the same Greek word that describes what Jesus did on the cross also describes what He is doing in our hearts — He is *crying. Krazo* is also used in John 12:44 when Jesus cries out about the oneness of Himself and the Father. And it is used again in John 7:37 when He cries out to call people to Himself: "Jesus stood and *cried out*, saying, If anyone thirsts, let him come to Me and drink." He cried out in a strong way.

*Krazo* is also used when John the Baptist cried out to introduce Jesus: "John testified concerning Him and *cried out,* saying, This was He of whom I said, He who is coming after me has become ahead of me, because He was before me" (John 1:15). He introduced the Lord with a *krazo*. Also in the Gospels the children were *crying out* and saying "Hosanna" in the temple (Matt. 21:15; John 12:13). They *krazoed*. They cried out. And in Mark 10:47 blind Bartimaeus *cried out* to Jesus for mercy. In Matthew 14:28-30 we see *krazo* used again when Peter began to sink while walking on the water: [28] "And Peter answered Him and said, Lord, if it is You, command me to come to You on the water. [29] And He said, Come. And Peter, coming down from the boat, walked on the water and came toward Jesus. [30] But seeing the strong wind, he became frightened; and as he began to sink, he *cried out,* saying, Lord, save me!" As he was sinking in the water, he *krazoed.*

In Acts 7:59-60 when Stephen was being stoned, both *epikaleo* and *krazo* were brought together in Stephen's experience: [59] "And they stoned Stephen as he called upon the Lord *[epikaleo],* and said, Lord Jesus, receive my spirit! [60] And kneeling down, he cried out *[krazo]* with a loud voice, Lord, do not hold this sin against them. And when he had said this, he fell asleep." Oh, I believe that prayer went to the throne and rebounded right back to Saul of Tarsus, who was standing there consenting to Stephen's death. Stephen *krazoed,* "Do not hold this sin against them," and it went right into Saul.

And we see the effects of that rebounding prayer when Saul was on the road to Damascus to further ravage the church. He was knocked to the ground by a light from heaven and, trembling and astonished, he said, "Lord, what do You want me to do?" (Acts 9:6). The answer came through a member of His Body. Ananias came to Saul and said, "Rise up and be baptized and wash away your sins, calling on His name" (Acts 22:16). It was as if the Lord was saying, "Now, Saul, you do what you have been persecuting others for doing. You were binding all those who were calling. Now I'm going to ask you to do what you didn't want to do — to call on My name."

And in Revelation 7:10 *krazo* is used again. The great multitude before the throne is *crying out* with a loud voice, saying, "Salvation to our God who sits upon the throne and to the Lamb." All these verses help us to see how much the Word of God is filled with calling and crying out upon the name of the Lord. This is the simplicity of staying in your spirit, drawing from the supply, staying in grace, staying out of yourself and out of your own energy. It is being a person who knows how to touch the spirit moment by moment and draw from the spirit, just in the concentration of His name. Brothers and sisters, all that we have ever shared about the Christian life or about the church life is now made real with one little handle, and that handle is "Jesus." It is all made real by that name and in that name, because that name is just His Person.

### *Breaking forth and shouting in Galatians 4:27*

There is another Greek word for crying out, shouting, and speaking with a strong voice. It is *boao*. This word is used in Mark 15:34 when Jesus was on the cross: "Jesus *cried* with a loud voice." And it is used to describe John the Baptist's ministry: "A voice of one *crying* in the wilderness, Prepare the way of the Lord; make straight His paths" (Matt. 3:3; cf. John 1:23). It is also used in Luke 18:1-8 about the saints continually praying to the Lord for His coming back: "His chosen ones, who *cry out* to Him day and night" (v. 7).

*Boao* is also used to describe the release resulting from the freedom of the new covenant in Galatians 4:27: "For it is written, Rejoice, barren one who does not bear; break forth and *shout,* you who are not travailing, because many are the children of her who is desolate rather than of her who has her husband." If there is no fruit in your life, if there is nothing that you have born — if this is your case — rejoice! This is what Paul speaks right in the middle of fellowshipping about the two covenants: the covenant from Mount Sinai and the covenant from the Jerusalem which is above. This is the new covenant versus the old covenant. The old covenant is about being under the law. The new covenant is about grace and about the realm of the spirit. It is a word that says, "Break forth and sing and shout." Why? Because something so wonderful has happened. This passage from Galatians is a quote out of Isaiah 54:1, which immediately follows chapter 53. There you discover that the Lord was "wounded for our transgressions," He was "bruised for our iniquities," and "the chastisement for our peace was upon Him." He has "borne our sicknesses and carried our sorrows" (vv. 4-5). He bore everything! So break forth and sing and shout!

### *Calling to experience all the benefits of Calvary*

What is unveiled in Isaiah 53 is the all-inclusiveness of the Lord's death on the cross. Jesus bore not only our sins, but our sorrows and our griefs and the chastisement and the judgment. He took it all. He suffered it all. He was punished. He was judged. Why? So that we would no longer be in that realm of bearing anything. He bore it all. Then Isaiah 54 starts out, "Break forth into singing, and cry aloud." See what He did at Calvary! You are carrying all that load. You are heavy laden. You are weighed down with burdens. You are bearing it all. Stop! He bore it all. Now you can break forth and shout! Release your spirit. Call upon the name of the Lord.

*Calling as the way to enter into God's thoughts*

Isaiah 55:6-9 says, [6] "Seek the LORD while He may be found, call upon Him while He is near. [7] Let the wicked forsake his way, and the unrighteous man his thoughts; let him return to the LORD, and He will have mercy on him; and to our God, for He will abundantly pardon. [8] 'For My thoughts are not your thoughts, nor are your ways My ways,' says the LORD. [9] 'For as the heavens are higher than the earth, so are My ways higher than your ways, and My thoughts than your thoughts.'" The Lord is saying, "Do you want to know My thoughts? I have just written them in Isaiah 53. I bore everything for you, and I have an abundance of mercy for you."

The thought here is, just turn to the Lord, and He will abundantly pardon: "For My thoughts are not your thoughts. Your thoughts are self-condemning thoughts. Your thoughts demean yourself. Your thoughts are so low — "There is no hope for me." Your thoughts are full of despair. Your thoughts are that you are not good enough. Your thoughts are that you have to wait for another day. Your thoughts are those kinds of thoughts. But My thoughts are not your thoughts. My thoughts are rooted in what I did in My Son on the cross. Those are My thoughts. With His stripes, you are healed." So now the good of it all is in calling upon Him while He is near. Just call upon the name of the Lord, and the good of all that He has done in the new covenant is your portion. It is all in the precious name of Jesus.

May the Lord indelibly inscribe in us the revelation of Himself and all that He has done — now concentrated in the name "Jesus." So when we speak that name, demons will flee, self is over, all of self's subjective state is terminated, and we get to participate in our God. "Thank You, Lord Jesus. Oh, we love You. We love Your name. We love the name that is above every name. Oh, Hallelujah. We just love to say Your precious name, Jesus, Jesus, Jesus. We praise Your name. You said that all those who believe on Your name will not be ashamed. We bow our knee. We confess with our tongue that Jesus Christ is Lord, to the glory of God the Father."

## 6 ▶ The History of Calling
## Upon the Name of the Lord

It is wonderful for us to see from the Word of God how much calling upon the name of the Lord was the pathway that so many saints took in the past. If we trace their path from the very beginning, it will be an overwhelming revelation to see in how many circumstances and environments the saints called upon the name of the Lord. It is so infusing to see from the Word the variety of ways the saints called upon His name.

*The first occasion of calling*
*upon the name of the Lord*

In studying the Bible it is always instructive to observe the first mention of any event, experience, or truth. This kind of observation has been called *the principle of first mention* by students of the Word. Whenever something is mentioned for the first time in the Word, it is helpful to see the principle of *how* it is mentioned. With this in mind, let us consider the first mention of calling upon the name of the Lord. It is found in Genesis 4:25-26: [25] "And Adam knew his wife again, and she bore a son and named him Seth, 'For God has appointed another seed for me instead of Abel, whom Cain killed.' [26] And as for Seth, to him also a son was born; and he named him Enosh. Then men began to *call on the name of the LORD*."

This is Genesis chapter 4. God had created man, and then the enemy came in to frustrate that creation. But the Lord came back to recover His purpose with man, that is, that man would express Him with His image and have His dominion. God had declared this purpose in Genesis chapter 1. But we know that sin came in, and man fell and was separated from God; and apparently God's purpose fell to the ground. Cain rose up and killed his brother, Abel. This was something so negative against God's purpose. But God raised up another seed, Seth. Seth means "set" or "fixed." This shows us that God was set upon carrying out His purpose despite the enemy's frustration.

Then to Seth, Enosh was born. In Hebrew Enosh means "weak and frail." This name actually has several definitions, another of which is "incurably sick and desperately wicked." That is the meaning of the name Enosh. It is a person who is weak and frail, desperately wicked and incurably sick. So here is man in this kind of state and then Genesis 4:26 says, "Then men began to call on the name of the LORD." Again, this is the first mention in the Bible of someone calling upon the name of the Lord. And it is interesting to see the atmosphere and the environment of that call: it is when man is weak, when man is frail, and when man is incurably sick. Nevertheless, God's purpose has not changed. And now to fulfill that purpose of being conformed to the image of Christ and having dominion over the enemy, there just needs to be a group of people who will begin to call upon the name of the Lord.

### *Abraham*

If you follow all the saints who were carrying out God's purpose, who were fulfilling what God wanted on this earth, you can see that they were those who called upon the name of the Lord. Now let us look at Abraham in Genesis chapter 12. God's purpose was over him. He had come out of Ur of the Chaldeans and now he was in the land of Canaan. Verse 8 says, "And he moved from there to the mountain east of Bethel, and he pitched his tent with Bethel on the west and Ai on the east; there he built an altar to the

LORD and called on the name of the LORD."

After we see men beginning to call with Enosh, we come to the example of Abraham setting up an altar and calling upon the name of the Lord. Whenever there is an altar, it means everything goes on that altar. There is some burning that is going on. There is some odor that is rising up as a sweet smelling savor to the Lord, and the Lord is satisfied. The Lord is pleased with what is offered on that altar, because it indicates that man is just living for God's good pleasure. That altar means we are offering ourself and we are living for God's good pleasure. For this to be our experience, we need the Lord Himself. So with the altar comes calling upon the name of the Lord.

After Abraham's altar experience, there was a famine in the land, and he went down to Egypt where he got into trouble. He found himself in a very awkward situation and he lied (Gen. 12:10-20). After being sent on his way, he returned back to the good land and back to the place where he had built the altar. Genesis 13:4 says that he came "to the place of the altar which he had made there at first. And there Abram called on the name of the LORD." So he initially called on the Lord, but later he got into trouble; and now he came back to calling again. It is the same with us.  Sometimes we may call, but then later we get into our self.  But we can come right back to calling upon the name of the Lord.

### Isaac

After Abraham there is Isaac.  In Genesis 26 Isaac is digging the wells that the Philistines had stopped up.  And the Lord appeared to him and made an oath with him. Then verse 25 says, "So he built an altar there and called on the name of the LORD, and he pitched his tent there; and there Isaac's servants dug a well."  Here Isaac is in the good land, in the same territory his father Abraham had dwelt.  And he too builds an altar and calls on the name of the Lord. Brothers and sisters, this is a line of callers — all the saints of God in the history of God's move, all those living for God's good pleasure, were those who called on the name of the Lord.

### Moses, Aaron, and Samuel

Deuteronomy 4:7 is a precious verse: "For what great nation is there that has God so near to it, as the LORD our God is to us, whensoever we call upon

Him." The last part of this verse can be translated "for whatever reason we may call upon Him." This is Moses' testimony concerning calling on the Lord. He says, "What nation is there whose God is so near as the LORD is to us, whenever or for whatever reason we may call upon Him." This shows us that the way to bring in the nearness of the Lord is just by opening our mouth to call that precious name, Jesus. This is how the Lord is near to us. It is just by the mention of His name.

Psalm 99:6 is another Old Testament verse about calling on the Lord. It says, "Moses and Aaron were among His priests, and Samuel was among those who called upon His name; they called upon the LORD, and He answered them." Here is a group of people who called upon the name of the Lord, and Moses, Aaron, and Samuel were among them. This means there is a group of people that we need to be among. There is a category of saints in the Bible known as the ones who call upon the name of the Lord. Not only in the New Testament do we find this category of those who were calling, but here in the Old Testament this verse tells us that Moses and Aaron and Samuel were among those who called upon the name of the Lord.

Praise the Lord that we could be in this line — the line of saints from the Old Testament and the line of saints in the New Testament. The Lord is recovering in our experience together the preciousness of calling upon that name. This calling comes out of a revelation of our absolute dependence upon God. Calling upon the name of the Lord inwardly means that I am a dependent man. I do not live my own life. I do not make my own moves. It is the Lord Jesus who is my life and who is my source. And I have a practical way to enjoy the source of the Lord in my being — it is by calling upon His name.

### *Samson*

In Judges 15 Samson was thirsty after his battle with the Philistines. Verses 18-19 say, [18] "Then he became very thirsty; so he *cried out* to the LORD and said, You have given this great deliverance by the hand of Your servant; and now shall I die of thirst and fall into the hand of the uncircumcised? [19] So God split the hollow place that is in Lehi, and water came out, and he drank; and his spirit returned, and he revived. Therefore he called its name En Hakkore, which is in Lehi to this day." The word "En Hakkore" literally means "the spring of the caller." God had provided a spring for this thirsty caller. So Samson's spirit returned and he was revived. This indicates that in this Old Testament saint's experience, he was crying out to the Lord to be refreshed.

## *David*

We know the testimony of David and how he called upon the name of the Lord. In 2 Samuel 22:4, after the Lord had delivered him from the hand of all his enemies and from the hand of Saul, he says, "I will call upon the LORD, who is worthy to be praised; so shall I be saved from my enemies." And again in verse 7 he says, "In my distress I called upon the LORD, and cried to my God. He heard my voice from His temple, and my cry entered His ears." And Psalm 116 is filled with David's calling upon the Lord. In verse 2 he says, "Therefore I will call upon Him as long as I live." And in verses 12-13 he says, [12] "What shall I render to the LORD for all His benefits toward me? [13] I will take up the cup of salvation, and call upon the name of the LORD." Not only with

David, but all through the Old Testament there is the testimony of saints calling upon the name of the Lord.

## THE PROPHETS

### *A pure language*

Zephaniah 3:9 is a precious verse showing what the Lord is recovering in the last days: "For then I will restore to the peoples a pure language [or, a pure lip], that they all may call on the name of the LORD, to serve Him with one accord." This verse does not leave us wondering what the pure language or the pure lip means. It specifically tells us what it is: "that they all may call on the name of the LORD." And then this calling on the Lord brings in serving Him with one accord. It brings in the oneness. It brings in the one shoulder to bear things together.

### *The remnant calling the Lord's name*

In Zechariah 13:9 the Lord says, "I will bring the one-third through the fire, will refine them as silver is refined, and test them as gold is tested. They will call on My name, and I will answer them. I will say, This is My people; and each one will say, The LORD is my God." This word in Zechariah tells us that out of all the refining, out of all the testing, there is a testimony. The purpose of the refining and the testing is to reduce us to the simplicity of enjoying the Lord Himself by calling on His name, and out of that comes the testimony: "I will say, This is My people; and each one will say, The Lord is my God." We come to know Him and enjoy Him by calling on His name.

### *Those who do not call*

As we consider this line of all the saints in the Old Testament who called upon the name of the Lord, we find that the Bible also mentions those who did not call. Let us see how the Holy Spirit speaks about those who refused to call. Psalm 14:4 says, "Have all the workers of iniquity no knowledge, who eat up my people as they eat bread, and do not call on the LORD?" Then Psalm 79:6 says, "Pour out Your wrath on the nations that do not know You, and on the kingdoms that do not call on Your name." Here again is the mention of those who do not call. Also Hosea 7:7 describes those who do not call: "They are all hot, like an oven, and have devoured their judges; all their kings have fallen. There is none among them who calls upon Me." None among them calls upon the Lord.

The Bible takes note of those who call and those who do not call. This is a testimony in the Word of God. So, brothers and sisters, it is not a small thing to be a person on this earth lifting up your voice and opening your mouth to call upon the name of the Lord. To be in the category of those who do not call means that we are not dependent, we are not instantly drawing from Another life. We are trusting in ourselves. We are trusting in our own abilities rather than being a person so dependent that we could be identified as one who calls upon the name of the Lord.

# 7 ◗ Calling Upon the Lord and Our Inward Parts

*Regeneration and calling upon His name*

We need to see the relationship between calling and our inward parts — how our spirit is so much connected to our calling upon the name of Jesus. We know initially that our spirit needs to be born, regenerated. This organ that God has put within us needs to actually experience resurrection, coming out of death into life. Our spirit must be born of God. And it is birthed when we open our mouth and speak the name "Jesus." Romans 10:13 says, "Whoever calls upon the name of the Lord shall be saved." When we call, that moment, that instant, our spirit is born. It is made alive. This is because this part of our being loves and feeds and saturates itself in the name of Jesus. This spirit of ours, with Christ living within, is waiting for that name to be spoken out of our mouth. Why? Because that name matches this inner, regenerated part that contains the life of God. So we can see this relationship — calling upon the name of the Lord with our mouth is intimately bound up with our spirit.

We may know about living in spirit, being filled in spirit, and walking according to spirit. For example, when you go to the store, you buy according to spirit. And when you are talking to your husband, you talk according to spirit. When you are making plans, you do it according to spirit. You purpose according to spirit (Acts 19:21). We are to be persons living in this realm. But we need a handle. This all may be just so much knowledge to us, but the handle to experience it is this precious name, the name of Jesus.

Speaking this name with our mouth is the way we control our whole being. The book of James makes this clear. James says that the tongue among our members is like the rudder of a ship and is like the bit in a horse's mouth (3:3-4). So here are all my members. My mind is a member. My emotions are a member. My eyes and ears are members. My body is made up of many members. All these things are part of me. They are all members of me. But there is one member among all the members that controls the rest, and that is the tongue.

As the rudder controls the ship and as the bit tames the horse, so the tongue controls our members. Your emotions may be going in a certain direction.

And your mind may be going in another direction. These members want to go with the wind or just be wild like a wild horse. How do you handle these members? Praise the Lord for our mouth: "If you confess with your mouth, Lord Jesus, and believe in your heart that God has raised Him from the dead, you will be saved" (Rom. 10:9). You will be saved from your feelings, saved from your reaction, saved from so many things. Our being is controlled by the name of Jesus being spoken out of our mouth.

## Calling and the presence of life

Calling upon the Lord is an evidence of the presence of life. This is a very encouraging point. Psalm 80:18 says, "Then we will not turn back from You; revive us, and we will call upon Your name." The Hebrew word "revive" means "give life." So some translations say, "Give us life and we will call upon Your name." This shows us that calling upon the Lord is the evidence of the presence of life. Calling means there is life in us. We can call upon the name of the Lord because there is life. Also there is life in that name (John 20:31). So when we are revived, when we are given life, we are surely the ones calling upon the name of the Lord.

## *Calling or coping?*

Ephesians 5:18-20 shows us the relationship between the filling of our spirit and the Lord's name: [18] "And do not be drunk with wine, in which is dissoluteness, but be filled in spirit, [19] speaking to one another in psalms and hymns and spiritual songs, singing and psalming with your heart to the Lord, [20] giving thanks at all times for all things in the name of our Lord Jesus Christ to our God and Father." Also in Isaiah 12 we see the relationship between the Lord's name and being filled in our spirit. Verses 3-4 say, [3] "Therefore with joy you will draw water from the wells of salvation. [4] And in that day you will say: Praise the LORD, call upon His name; declare His deeds among the peoples, make mention that His name is exalted."

Now let us look at some verses that show us that the things existing in our heart become reality by calling upon His name. Romans 10:8-9 says, [8] But what does it say? 'The word is near you, in your mouth and in your heart,' that is, the word of the faith which we proclaim, [9] that if you confess *with your mouth* Jesus as Lord and believe in your heart that God has raised Him from the dead, you will be saved." In verse 9 the order starts with your mouth. This is because there is already something in your heart. In your heart you believe. You do believe. There is an infusion there — the word of faith. So what do you do with what is in your heart? The order in Romans chapter 10 is that if you will confess with your mouth and believe in your heart you will be saved. The order is the mouth taking the lead to release what is in your heart.

But so many times you are just bottled up. You have so much inside. There is so much mind activity going on. You are coping. You are striving. Inwardly you are trying to handle yourself. But you were not made to handle yourself. You were made to call upon the name of the Lord. "Jesus!" When you call you get out of that coping mode. Your blood pressure goes down. And you get normalized because He is the Handler. He is the Savior. He is the Lord.

We are simply learning in one thing at a time — in one environment at a time, in one reaction at a time — not to go out and meet that, not to go out and interact with it, not to go out and try to change ourself. We are learning that simple word, "Come unto Me all you who labor. Come unto Me, you who are burdened." We are just learning in our experience how to stop ourself and come to the Lord and bring whatever to Him. We realize we don't have to handle it. We don't have to interact with it. But the way this happens is by speaking that name, "Jesus." It is by His name that we stop ourself from all this energy, and then our spirit is filled up and our heart is filled up.

## *Finding Christ with your mouth*

In Romans 10:6-10 we see how we find Christ within us — it is with our mouth: 6 "But the righteousness which is out of faith speaks in this way, Do not say in your heart, Who will ascend into heaven? that is, to bring Christ down; 7 or, Who will descend into the abyss? that is, to bring Christ up from the dead. 8 But what does it say? The word is near you, in your mouth and in your heart, that is, the word of the faith which we proclaim, 9 that if you confess *with your mouth* Jesus as Lord and believe in your heart that God has raised Him from the dead, you will be saved; [10] for with the heart there is believing unto righteousness, and with the mouth there is confession unto salvation." Find Christ within you with your mouth.

Then we see the relationship between calling and faith in Romans 10:14-17. Faith is infused into us, and calling is just the expression of that faith that is infused into us. And Romans 10:3-17 clearly reveals that calling brings Christ into us as a gift rather than as a reward for works. So you realize how you and I get saved. It is not by our works. It is nothing we can do. Yet we can call upon the name of the Lord. And the moment we call upon the name of the Lord, we are saved. So the gift of life is given to us when we stop our works and our energy, and the only thing we are doing is calling "Jesus." And in that name He dispenses life into us and gives us the gift of righteousness. This is the way we get saved. And it is not only the way we get saved; it is also the way we go on. Calling preserves our experience of Christ in the realm of grace. We remain in grace rather than slipping into our own efforts. This is how to stay in the realm of grace — stay in the realm of receiving. And this is by speaking His name.

*His name and the dividing of soul and spirit*

Now let us see the relationship between confessing His name and the dividing of soul and spirit. Through the book of Hebrews there is a recurring phrase: "Hold fast the confession." It is just that simple expression. In chapter 2 we do not yet see everything put under Him, but we see Jesus (v. 8). We just see Jesus. And our confession is just Jesus. Hold fast the confession. And when we hold fast that confession, there is a dividing of soul and spirit. That is how you get divided. We have seen it happen again and again where there has been an enmeshing of the soul and spirit, and no dividing. You are one big ball of condemnation and horrible feelings and introspection and looking at yourself and being inwardly all bound up. You are just all enmeshed. And the enemy is all enmeshed in there. How do you get out of it? It is by "Jesus." It is by His name. It is a deep call, where everything gets flushed out. And then you come up with Him and in Him, and you are objective in your spirit over this thing called self and the way it acts and reacts. And you speak to it and put it in its right place. This is by the name of Jesus. It is a dividing that comes by the name.

## *The name of Jesus and the oneness of the church*

How could we as believers come into such organic oneness as Paul describes in 1 Corinthians 1:10? Here he says, "that you all speak the same thing and that there be no divisions among you, but that you be perfectly attuned in the same mind and in the same opinion." The way Paul appeals to the saints to come into this oneness is *through the name:* "I beseech you through the name of the Lord Jesus that you would be one." This is not just a religious way of thinking. I believe he was referring back to what he said in verse 2: "To the church of God which is in Corinth, to those who have been sanctified in Christ Jesus, the called saints, with all those who are *calling upon the name* of our Lord Jesus Christ in every place, who is theirs and ours." The word "calling" is in the present tense. It is not that these saints just called once. The church was a group of ones who called on His name.

So in verse 10 Paul touches the problem of division by revealing to the saints that their oneness is by that name. Our calling upon that name, our touching that name, just filters out all the divisiveness, all the walls that separate us. One of the brothers testified that after a wall had come between his wife and him, they just called "Jesus" together. That was a bowing. And that was a harmony. Their calling brought in the oneness together, even without saying so much. When we call the name of Jesus, many times we don't explain that much. We are just brought into the reality of the name. So calling on the name of the Lord is related to the church and the oneness of the church.

*Enjoying the name and the organic church life*

The phrase "the generality of the church" has been used to describe the proper standing of a local church. It means we stand together as the church in our locality on a common ground to receive all brothers and sisters regardless of our backgrounds, regardless of what differences there may be. The church must be standing on a ground that includes all born-again believers. This is what Watchman Nee ministered in China years ago. Later it was published in the book *The Normal Christian Church Life*. Again, to actually meet on this common ground requires that we receive all saints, that we are open to all believers.

Of course, we know that all believers are not assembling with us. Nevertheless, our standing is to receive all. This is the proper standing of the church. And in this standing we must practice what we have understood as the generality among the saints. In Romans 14 we see that Paul practiced this generality. Among the believers some were eating meat and some were not eating meat. Some were esteeming one day above another, and some were esteeming every day alike. To this Paul says, "Let every man be fully persuaded in his own mind" (v. 5). Even Paul does not try to settle an issue about whether or not to eat meat or whether to make the church a meat-eating church or a non-meat-eating church. Paul does not make that decision. He remains very general, saying, "Let every man be fully persuaded in his own mind," and "Receive one another, as Christ also received you to the glory of God" (15:7). This is what it means to practice the generality of the church.

The phrase "the speciality of the church" means that as believers we are not so general as to receive another gospel. In Galatians 1:8 Paul says, "But even if we, or an angel from heaven, preach any other gospel to you than what we have preached to you, let him be accursed." Thus, we are not so general as to receive some other so-called faith or some way other than Jesus. In this we are special, we are unique. We hold to "the faith once for all delivered to the saints" (Jude 3). This is our common salvation provided by the blood of Jesus, by His finished work, by His resurrection, and by our believing in the Triune God. All this is special — it is the speciality of the church.

But when it comes to different kinds of doctrines and even different practices, we have always held to what is known as the generality of the church. Yet that generality of the church has been tested and challenged among us. When personalities rose up and issues rose up, instead of practicing a generality to receive all saints, this was nullified by making those matters special that should have been treated as general. For some, the generality of the church was just a kind of doctrine to believe in, a teaching to be held, a principle to live by — "We need to be general." But when the test came, what happened to the generality? Why couldn't we receive all the saints to practice the church life according to each one's conscience and enjoyment of Christ and still have a sweet fellowship with no middle walls? What happened?

Well, I would say the generality of the church that is practiced must be understood not just as a doctrine, but as an organic reality. The generality of the church is the organic church life where we are organically joined together, preserving the oneness of the Spirit between us. To have the oneness of the Spirit between us is to be organic. It means this: Husband and wife, something happens between you. Reasoning comes in. Some words are said. Before this time, you were organic. It was comfortable. You could fellowship, and you could pray. You could open to one another. You could keep the oneness of the Spirit together even though you differed on some practical points in your life. You didn't allow your reasoning mind to step over the line to ruin that sweetness of the Spirit and the fellowship.

But when you come in with reasoning and super-impose something, it breaks the flow and the fellowship. This was what was happening among the saints in Rome. So Paul said to them, "The kingdom of God is not eating and drinking." It is not having your way about your own opinion. This is what eating and drinking signifies. But the kingdom of God is "righteousness and peace and joy in the Holy Spirit" (Rom. 14:17). So we can see that the generality of the church is not just holding a principle of meeting. It is keeping the oneness of the Spirit and the peace and the joy of the Spirit between us. It is preserving this.

The generality of the church is really the organic nature of preserving the Spirit. Paul prayed in Ephesians that the saints would be strengthened into their inner man, that Christ could settle down in their hearts. Why? So that they could be rooted and grounded in love. Why? To apprehend with all the saints and then to be led straight into Ephesians 4, where Paul says, "Be quick [or, diligent] to keep the oneness of the Spirit in the uniting bond of peace" (v. 3). Thus, the goal of Christ making home in our hearts is the oneness of the Body. When we are so strengthened into our inner man, so filled up with the fullness of God, we can together learn how to live organically in the oneness of the Spirit.

We are not perfect. We are imperfect. We are in the process. We make mistakes. There is shortness among us on occasions. We even offend one another. But we are strengthened into our inner man to learn to see beyond it all, to keep the oneness of the Spirit, and to not lose that drinking of the Spirit together, that calling together, that flowing together, despite whatever may happen. This is the reality.

In Romans 14 Paul knew how to get the saints together. He was getting the Jewish saints and the Gentile saints to meet together on a common ground in Rome for that kingdom life to be expressed. And in verses 5-7 of chapter 15 he says, [5] "Now the God of endurance and encouragement grant you to be of the same mind toward one another according to Christ Jesus, [6] that with one accord you may with one mouth glorify the God and Father of our Lord Jesus Christ. [7] Therefore receive one another, as Christ also received you to the glory of God." And then he goes on in verses 9-11: [9] "And that the Gentiles should glorify God for His mercy, as it is written, Therefore I will extol You among the Gentiles, and I will sing praise to Your name. [10] And again He says, Rejoice, Gentiles, with His people. [11] And again, Praise the Lord, all you Gentiles, and let all the peoples speak praise to Him."

So what Paul is doing here is just gathering the saints together and letting the saints praise the Lord and confess His name together. He knew that this is how you stay organic. It is by calling on that precious name, being brought into the Spirit and keeping the oneness of the Spirit in the bond of peace. The peace is God Himself. He is not for a method. He is not for a way. He is for Himself. And the peace in the Spirit is Himself. How wonderful that we can call upon the name of the Lord and enjoy the oneness of the church life together.

VARIOUS EXPERIENCES OF CALLING

### *Meeting the Lord in His name*

In the Bible there are many verses related to specific experiences of calling upon the name of the Lord. Isaiah 52:6-7 reveals the experience of meeting the Lord Himself in His name. Verse 6 says, "Therefore My people shall know My name; therefore they shall know in that day that I am He who speaks: Behold, it is I." This is what happens when we call upon the name of the Lord — we meet the Lord. It is as if He says, "Oh, here I am. Behold, it is I." That is the reality of calling upon the name of the Lord. When you call, inwardly you have that deep sense that the Lord is speaking, "Behold, it is I." Then verse 7 says, "How beautiful upon the mountains are the feet of him who brings good news, who proclaims peace, who brings glad tidings of good things, who proclaims salvation, who says to Zion,

Your God reigns!" This verse from Isaiah is quoted by Paul in Romans 10, where he speaks extensively about calling on the name of the Lord. The purpose of proclaiming peace and bringing the glad tidings is that the hearing ones can become the calling ones (cf. Rom. 10:14-15). Then the calling ones meet the Lord in their call.

## *Losing the self-life by His name*

In Romans 10:12 we see the losing of the self-life and all the prejudices by the name: "For there is no distinction between Jew and Greek, for the same Lord over all is rich to all who call upon Him." There is *no distinction* between Jew and Greek. Sometimes in coming to the church, some of the new brothers and sisters may feel they are not a part of us. They feel that the other saints have been here for so many years and have such a history together. This feeling of not being "a part" is a feeling of the flesh. You have to know this is what it is. It is a fleshly feeling. It comes out of the self and the soul, because in the new man there is neither Greek nor Jew. So when you get to the Spirit and call upon the name of the Lord, there is no difference between Jew and Greek.

Even if there may be some undealt-with things in a member, if you call "Jesus," you will not be related to that person according to his untransformed state. You will be brought into that oneness and that divine flow of love toward them, rather than living in a state of looking down at others, interpreting others, judging others — all in terms of yourself.

We have to see that there is no difference between Jew and Greek, for the same Lord of all is rich to all who call. Paul knew how to get the Jewish believers to meet together with the Gentile believers. And they were poles apart! How are you going to get them together in the meetings? There is *no difference* to all who call. It is in the precious name.

### *Becoming inaccessibly high by His name*

Psalm 20:1 says, "May the LORD answer you in the day of trouble; may the name of the God of Jacob defend you." Notice that it says, "may the name defend you." The Hebrew word "defend" means to cause you to become inaccessibly high so that you cannot be captured. So it could read, "May the name of the God of Jacob make you inaccessibly high so that you cannot be touched by the enemy." This is what the name of Jesus does. It brings us far above all, seated with Him in the heavenlies, inaccessibly high, out of the reach of the enemy. Oh, praise the Lord for His name!

May the Lord unveil the reality of His name far more than we could ever say by our human words. In all our environments and all our experiences, may we be ones discovering the riches of His person and the riches of what He has done. We can apply all these riches in the nitty-gritty details of our daily living just by learning to speak that name again and again. When we speak that name we connect with our spirit, and in that realm we become objective and can sort out everything that is not God. This is how we can all be in the church life together keeping the oneness. We know there is something between us, and what is between us is God Himself.

# 8 ▶ The Authority of the Name of Jesus

*The history behind the name of Jesus*

In Philippians 2:8-9 Paul says of the Lord, [8] "Being found in fashion as a man, He humbled Himself, becoming obedient even unto death, and that the death of a cross. [9] Therefore also God highly exalted Him and bestowed on Him the name which is above every name." The Lord received the name that is above every name as a gift bestowed by the Father based upon all that He passed through — His incarnation, His human living, His obedience, His death on the cross, His resurrection, and His exaltation. The coronation of all that process was the bestowing of the highest name upon Him. But this was not just an isolated event that occurred 2000 years ago in the heavens. Verses 10-11 tell us for what purpose He was given the name which is above every name: [10] "That at the name of Jesus every knee should bow, of those who are in heaven and on earth and under the earth, [11] and every tongue should openly confess that Jesus Christ is Lord to the glory of God the Father."

Now every knee bows at the name of Jesus. At the mention of that name, at the speaking of that name, there is the bowing and the confessing out that Jesus Christ is Lord to the glory of God the Father. When we speak that name, Jesus, there is authority in that name. Behind that name is all that He has accomplished. And behind that name and in that name is the defeat of the devil and every demon. And in that name is the victory over the flesh and the old man and the self. It is all overcome in that name.

> *The reactions of the soul and*
> *demons to the name of Jesus*

At the name of Jesus there is power and there is authority. So when you speak the name of Jesus and speak about the name of Jesus, you will discover something happening to you. You begin to tremble inside. You begin to react inside. You even find rebellion rising up within you like you have never known before. Why? Because before the bowing, comes the rising up of those things that are against the knowledge of God. It is important to observe that Satan, the enemy, and demonic thinking and soulishness are all enmeshed together. In the book of

James, the words "soulish" and "demonic" are put together. He speaks of a wisdom that is "earthly, soulish, demonic" (3:15). This means that in the soul there is the activity of the demonic things. Inordinate thinking, rebellion, resistance, indifference — all this is in the soul and is enmeshed with the enemy.

When we are living in our self, in our soul, oftentimes everything is at peace. We have our opinions, we are fortified in ourself, and everything is peaceful. This is the way Luke 11:21 describes the enemy: "When the strong man, fully armed, guards his own homestead, his possessions are in peace." The word "homestead" could be literally translated "courtyard." It is the facade of a residence. The courtyard is guarded by the strong man, and his possessions are in peace. This means that everything is tranquil. There seems to be no problem. Everything is there in a quiet state. Then verse 22 says, "But when one stronger than he comes upon him and overcomes him, he takes away his whole armor in which he had trusted and distributes his spoil." The One stronger than the strong man is Jesus. And the stronger One is that name, Jesus. When He comes upon the strong man, He shakes up everything, and that which was at peace begins to come to the surface and manifest itself for what it is.

## *Overthrowing the enmeshed enemy by the name of Jesus*

Paul speaks in 2 Corinthians 10:4 about the enemy's activity being like strongholds in us, like fortified cities that have been built up. These strongholds can be thought patterns, things in you and me where we have resisted the Lord. We have a view, we have a concept, we have a certain way of thinking, and it is holding us back from the release of Christ within us. These are like strongholds. They are built up. They are fortified. And when Paul talks about these strongholds, he doesn't just talk about pulling one little plank out at a time and taking them apart piece by piece. He talks about "overthrowing" strongholds. It could be likened to a bulldozer coming through and just pushing everything out.

Paul also speaks of overthrowing "every high thing rising up against the knowledge of God" (v. 5). Are there things rising up in you? That may be a sign that the enemy is getting shaken up inside. So when the name of Jesus is strong in the church, and the name of Jesus is strong on the earth, and the name of Jesus is strong in the heavens and under the earth, things are going to get shaken up where the enemy has been at peace, where Satan has enmeshed himself with the souls of men and everything has been quietly and deceptively under his control without God.

At the same time things are rising up, they are all getting ready for the bowing. Everything that rises up within us is just a prime target to bow. So when that resistance rises up, when those thoughts come up, when that stronghold comes up again, that is just the time for the enemy to be caught red-handed. He was at peace before. He was there hidden, enmeshed. So we were controlled by Satan, the enemy. He was just enmeshed there. But when a Stronger than he comes, He takes away everything that he trusted in.

When we call "Jesus," that is the bowing of our inner being to the headship of Christ. So do not be bothered by resistance in you. It is a sign that things are getting loosened up. The strongholds are beginning to shake so that at the name of Jesus every knee will bow and every tongue will confess out that Jesus Christ is Lord. Everything is in that name. The authority is in that name.

*Calling the name and the*
*dividing of soul and spirit*

That name is the practical way to touch our spirit. And we all know that to live the Christian life, we have to walk according to spirit. We have to interact with our spirit and know the Lord inwardly and touch Him inwardly. But how do we know Him inwardly apart from speaking that precious name? That name is the name that matches our spirit. It is the name that fits the interaction with the Lord in our spirit. When we speak that name, we touch the Spirit. And when we touch the Spirit, we get a dividing. We get a dividing of soul and spirit. There is an ability to identify things that have usurped us — "You usurping thing, you have fooled me, you have lied to me. You kept me in the grave, you deceiving liar. In Jesus name, get out of here." This is a dividing rather than merging with those thoughts, believing those thoughts, being controlled by those thoughts. Just imagine the pitiful state of being under satanic, demonic thinking right within your soul, being under a thinking that resists the Lord.

This is why just at the name of Jesus — not even with a message from the Word, not even with knowledge, but just at the name Jesus — all the powers of darkness are shaken up and you and I feel it. Those reactions are not just your reactions. It is that strong man who was at peace but who has been shaken up at that name. But he has been shaken up so that he can come out of the shadows, and we have him as a target now. He wasn't a target before. He was hiding. The enemy hides. The serpent is sneaky. He hides in your thoughts, he hides in your strongholds. He is hiding there. But at the name of Jesus every knee bows, and then we experience the dividing of soul and spirit.

First Corinthians 2:11 says, "For who among men knows the things of man, except the spirit of man which is in him? In the same way, the things of God also no one has known except the Spirit of God." In this verse it is categorically clear that we cannot know ourselves in the realm of the soul. The realm of knowing ourselves is the spirit. Who knows the things of man? Who knows your condition? Who knows your real state? Who knows where you really are? How do you know yourself? What do you trust? What do you live by? What controls you? How do we know ourself? Who knows the things of man, except the spirit of man which is in him?

The fastest way to the spirit of man is "Jesus." In that name, Jesus, we are according to spirit. We are in spirit. We are touching the spirit. And it is from the spirit that enlightenment comes to know the things of ourselves — to know our soul, to know that this thought is from Satan, to know that this is the self, to know that this is the old man, to know that this is the flesh. We have to get it out there to see it. Otherwise, we are enmeshed with it — we live under it, we believe it, and we are controlled by it. So we have to get it out in front of us. But we cannot do this by knowledge or by all our past experiences or by any other way. We can only do it by today's present touch with the spirit.

## *Sorting ourselves out by calling the name*

Who knows the things of man, except the spirit of man which is in him? It is our spirit that knows us. So when you touch the spirit, you get objective about yourself. Instead of sinking subjectively into your own thoughts, into your own feelings — "What are they thinking about me?" — we quickly sort everything out. Let me give an illustration. I have an abundance of information in the databases of my computer. And I just enjoy going into my database program and clicking "sort." When I am looking for something specific, I just enter it on the screen and click the "sort" button. All I have to do is touch that one button and everything gets sorted. That is like touching our spirit. When you touch the spirit, you get "sorted." Everything gets sorted out. The flesh is sorted out, the devil is sorted out, and you know who you are. All this happens at the name of Jesus — just by touching the spirit.

Proverbs 20:27 says, "The spirit of a man is the lamp of the LORD, searching all the inner depths of his heart." Or another translation says, "searching all the inner parts of the belly." This verse shows us that the spirit of man is the place from which everything is searched out. So when we are in our spirit we know ourself, and in knowing ourself we get to know the Lord. To really know the Lord is to know ourself. And you cannot know yourself apart from knowing Him, because it is in His light that we see light. Jeremiah 17:9 says, "The heart is deceitful above all things, and desperately wicked; who can know it?" Who can sort the heart out? Then verse 10 says, "I, the LORD, search the heart." The Lord is the heart-knower. So to know ourself — to live not by ourself, but by God — we have to touch the realm of the spirit.

Who knows the things of a man, except the spirit of man? Don't trust in your puny thoughts about yourself. You don't really know yourself. I don't really know myself. For man to really, thoroughly, know himself, he must be in his spirit. And the name of Jesus yokes us instantly with our spirit. When you call from deep within, "Jesus," right away you get sorted. You find out who is who and what is what. The clarity comes in our spirit, and our spirit is yoked to that name. It is in the realm of the spirit that you get to know yourself and you see yourself and you can laugh at yourself. You can laugh at how pathetic it is. You can call yourself a monster and be altogether objective about it.

In Ezekiel chapter 36 the Lord opens up the new covenant to us: "I will give you a new heart and put a new spirit within you; I will take the heart of stone out of your flesh and give you a heart of flesh. I will put My Spirit within you and cause you to walk in My statutes, and you will keep My judgments and do them" (vv. 26-27). Right after these verses about a new heart and a new spirit, the Lord shows us another part of the new covenant: "You will loathe your-selves" (v. 31). So the ability to loathe yourself is a gift of the grace that comes from your spirit. You are able by this grace to be so objective about yourself—to say to your wife, "Honey, sorry, that monster just talked to you a few minutes ago," and then you go right on with God.

This is because in the Spirit we can call the self for what it is. You know what it is. Instead of being in a false relationship with one another, you can be transparent, you can be open, you can talk about God in each other. You can lay down your soul-life. You can apologize. You can admit. You can be honest. You can open up without a chip on your shoulder — no inferiorities. Inferiority only comes when you are enmeshed with the enemy somewhere in your mind. It produces in you self-introspection: "I'm no good, I'm so worthless." This is all the enemy. But just call "Jesus" and you get objective real quick. You are catapulted out of that subjectivity into an objective state about your being, and you lose that soul-life. Like Paul you will say, "I know that in me, that is, in my flesh, nothing good dwells" (Rom. 7:18).

*The realm of the Spirit and the name of Jesus*

The realm of the Spirit is connected to the name of Jesus. We see this in Paul's experience: "And having the same spirit of faith according to that which is written, 'I believed, therefore I spoke,' we also believe, therefore we also speak" (2 Cor. 4:13). This is the same pattern that is in Romans 10:10, where Paul says that with the heart there is believing and with the mouth there is confession. In this passage from 2 Corinthians Paul is quoting David from Psalm 116 and saying that we have the same spirit of faith that David had. That means resident in our spirit is faith. We have a spirit of faith. So within our being is everything we need. It is here.

We have the spirit of faith. I believe. Do you believe? I believe, regardless of how I feel right now, regardless of where my mind is, regardless of my will. I may even feel resistant to the Lord. But regardless of that, I believe. Deeper than my mind, deeper than my feelings, deeper than my will, there is a life resident in my spirit. Faith is there resident in my spirit. I believe. But the key to believing is "I speak." So just break up the logjam. There is a logjam in your mind. There is a logjam in your emotions. Just break it up by the life of the Spirit flowing out with your speaking. We believe, therefore we speak.

Let us look at David's experience in Psalm 116. In verses 3-4 he says, [3] "The pains of death encompassed me, and the pangs of Sheol laid hold of me; I found trouble and sorrow. [4] Then I called upon the name of the LORD: O LORD, I implore You, deliver my soul!" So David was speaking by calling. Then in verses 5-11 he says, [5] "Gracious is the LORD, and righteous; yes, our God is merciful. [6] The LORD preserves the simple; I was brought low, and He saved me. [7] Return to your rest, O my soul" — return to that realm where there is rest from all that turmoil in the soul — "for the LORD has dealt bountifully with you. [8] For You have delivered my soul from death, my eyes from tears, and my feet from falling. [9] I will walk before the LORD in the land of the living. [10] I believed, therefore I spoke, I am greatly afflicted. [11] I said in my haste, All men are liars." This was how David reacted to his environment. He said in his haste, "All men are liars." But then he says, [12] "What shall I render to the LORD for all His benefits toward me? [13] I will take up the cup of salvation, and call upon the name of the LORD." How do we react to our environment? Take the cup of salvation and call upon the name of the Lord.

### *The realm of death and resurrection operating in the name of Jesus*

In 2 Corinthians chapter 4 Paul is talking about his experiences, how he was hard-pressed on every side and persecuted and struck down (vv. 8-9). He was passing through all these things, but he wasn't crushed, he wasn't forsaken, he wasn't destroyed. He was passing through all these things, but somehow he was coming through. Death was working in him, and resurrection life was coming out. So here is a man experiencing death and resurrection: death to the self-life, death to that self-pity, death to all that morbid introspection that would come as a result of being under so many problems. Paul was putting to death. He says, "We who are alive are always being delivered unto death for Jesus' sake that the life of Jesus also may be manifested in our mortal flesh" (v. 11).

Paul was always being handed over to death for Jesus' sake. The putting to death of Jesus was always in him that the life of Jesus would keep coming out. But what is the handle to it all? How do you experience this, Paul? How does it actually happen? He tells us — "death operates in us, but life in you." And then he immediately adds in verse 13, "And having the same spirit of faith according to that which is written, 'I believed, therefore I spoke,' we also believe, therefore we also speak." When you look at the content of what Paul spoke, you discover that he was taking the cup of salvation and calling upon the name of the Lord. That is what he spoke. He spoke "Jesus," which brought him into the realm of the Spirit and caused him to be so transformed. He was transformed experience after experience by the name that is above every name.

So, brothers and sisters, all we need is the name of Jesus. In that name is His person. And when you speak that name you will shake up the enemy. Despite your feelings, what you think, or your past experiences — deeply call from within. Or if you are in a situation where you are bothered by others, just call "Jesus" with your whole heart and from deep within. That name is attached to everything He is. That name is attached to all that He is and all that He has done. You will discover a breakthrough to the overthrowing of strongholds so that you get divided. The spirit and the soul will be separated rather than being enmeshed, and you will not be under the cloud of your thoughts and intimidated by that whispering going on in your mind about yourself and against yourself. Your spirit and soul are all enmeshed because you won't open your mouth. As long as you won't put your foot down and take the good land — which is an Old Testament picture of Christ — you will be given over to your enemies. God will let them chase you. They are chasing you all over the place. But the moment you put your foot down by calling "Jesus!" the Lord says, "I will put them to flight now." He will chase all those enemies away. You don't have to live the way you are living. It is not normal. You don't have to live that way. It's all in the name of Jesus.

### *Overthrow reasonings and catch the thoughts*

In 2 Corinthians 10:4-5 Paul says that when we overthrow the strongholds of reasonings, we will be able to catch every thought and bring it "unto the obedience of Christ." We may have thought that we needed to catch every thought first. But how am I going to catch all these things going by? They are coming because there is a stronghold there. First, overthrow the stronghold. Get divided and then you start catching these little thoughts that come into your mind. You are no longer under the intimidation of the enemy. Oh, Satan hates that you would experience this, because when you do, you come to the church meeting and you supply Christ. You are not there thinking about yourself, worried about yourself. You have thrown off your self, and the church gets the benefit. Death works in us, and life goes to the Body.

The name of Jesus is above every name. He was crowned with the highest name. The Father gave Him that name. He won it. He earned it by His humanity passing through the victory all those years and going into resurrection. Now He is given a name that is above every name. But it is not just so that Jesus can have a trophy, so to speak, in His trophy case. Being given the highest name is not an end in itself. Now at that name every knee bows and every tongue confesses. So let us call upon the Lord out of a pure heart. Just "Jesus." Deliberately, "Jesus, Jesus, Jesus. We love Your name. We speak Your name. Release Your name in every mouth so that every knee will bow and every tongue will confess that Jesus Christ is Lord."

# 9 ▶ A Summary Outline of Calling Upon the Name of the Lord

## I. The Significance of a Name in the Bible

A. The name stands for the person – Acts 1:15; Rev. 3:4; Num. 26:53, 55

  1. To know the name is to know the person – 1 Sam. 25:25; Psa. 9:10

B. The name expresses the nature of a thing or person

  1. Adam naming the animals – Gen. 2:19-20

  2. Adam naming "Eve" – Gen. 3:20

C. Changing a name meant changing a person's character, status, and destiny

  1. Abram to Abraham – Gen. 17:4-5

  2. Jacob to Israel – Gen. 32:27-28

  3. Simon to Peter – Matt. 16:17-18

D. The name of Jesus and what He does – Matt. 1:21

## II. The Revelation of God in His Names

A. *Elohim* (The almighty creating God) – Gen. 1:1; Rom. 4:17; Heb. 11:3

B. *Jehovah / Yahweh* (The self-existent, becoming One) – Exo. 3:13-14; 6:3; John 8:58

C. *El-Shaddai* (The almighty nourishing,
   satisfying, and supplying One)
   – Gen. 17:1-2; Psa. 91:1
D. *Adonai* (Lord, master, owner)
   – Psa. 16:2; Acts 2:36
E. *Jehovah-jireh* (I AM provides)
   – Gen. 22:8, 14; Phil. 4:19
F. *Jehovah-rapha* (I AM heals)
   – Exo. 15:26; James 5:14-16
G. *Jehovah-nissi* (I AM, my banner)
   – Exo. 17:15-16; 2 Cor. 2:14
H. *Jehovah-qadash* (I AM sanctifies)
   – Exo. 31:13; Lev. 20:8; 1 Thess. 5:23
I. *Jehovah-tsidkenu* (I AM, our righteousness)
   – Jer. 23:6; 33:16; 1 Cor. 1:30
J. *Jehovah-shalom* (I AM is peace)
   – Judg. 6:24; Eph. 2:14
K. *Jehovah-shammah* (I AM is there)
   – Ezek. 48:35
L. The revelation of His name and calling
   – Jer. 33:2-3

## III. The Economy and Process of the Name
A. The name inherited in eternity past
   – Heb. 1:2-4; Col. 1:16-17

B. The name *Jehovah* in the Old Testament and the name *Jesus* in the New Testament – John 8:24, 28, 58 (cf. Exo. 3:13-14; Rev. 1:4)

C. The name at the incarnation – Matt. 1:21, 23; Isa. 9:6

D. The name during His human living – Heb. 4:14-16

E. The name through crucifixion – Heb. 2:9-10

F. The name through burial – Acts 2:27, 31-32; 1 Pet. 3:18-22; Eph. 4:9-10

G. The name in resurrection – Eph. 1:19-21

H. The name in exaltation – Phil. 2:9-11

I. The significance of the bestowal of the name which is above every name – Phil. 2:9

J. The name given to the church – Eph. 1:19-23

K. Jesus is Lord and Christ – Acts 2:33-36

L. The response to the name – Phil. 2:10-11; Isa. 45:21-25

M. The universal position of the name – Acts 4:12

N. The Lord's person and work concentrated in His name – 1 Cor. 6:11

O. The way to touch the riches of the Lord's person and finished work – Rom. 10:12-13; Acts 22:16

## IV. The Relationship between the Lord as the Spirit and His Name

A. The relationship between the Lord as the Spirit and His name – John 14:16-20, 26; 1 Cor. 6:11

B. The sending of the Spirit and the Lord's name – John 14:26

C. Life from Christ as the life-giving Spirit in His name – 1 Cor. 15:45; John 20:31

D. The name and being in the Holy Spirit – 1 Cor. 12:3, 13

E. The Lord's name and the Lord's doing – John 14:13-14

## V. The Meaning of the Word "Calling" in the Bible

A. The Hebrew word *qara* (קָרָא)

1. Call, cry, utter a loud sound (Isa. 36:13)
2. Call unto someone (Psa. 57:2)
3. Cry for help like a raven (Psa. 147:9)
4. Invite and summon someone (Isa. 55:6)

B. The Greek word *epikaleo* (ἐπικαλέω)

1. To call to; to call upon; to appeal to
2. To call out; to cry out upon
3. To surname or designate someone

4. The Greek preposition *epi* (ἐπί), prefixed to the root word *kaleo* (καλέω), emphasizes the object called upon.

5. The Greek verb *epikaleo*, when related to calling on the name of the Lord, is always used in the middle voice in the New Testament. The active voice stresses the action itself; the passive voice stresses the subject being acted upon; whereas, the middle voice stresses the agent or subject involved and participating in the verbal action. (Examples: the present middle – Acts 7:59; 9:14, 21; Rom. 10:12; 1 Cor. 1:2; 2 Tim. 2:22; 1 Pet.1:17; the aorist middle – Acts 2:21; 22:16; Rom. 10:13; the future middle – Rom. 10:14)

C. The Greek word for "crying"— *krazo* (κράζω)

1. To cry; to cry out; cry aloud

2. Speak with a loud voice; shriek like a raven

3. Crying "Abba, Father" – Gal. 4:6; Rom. 8:15-16 (cf. Mark 14:36)

4. Jesus crying out about Himself and the Father – John 12:44

5. Jesus crying out to call people to Himself – John 7:37

6. The Lord crying out on the cross
   – Matt. 27:50-51

7. John the Baptist crying out to introduce
   Jesus – John 1:15

8. Peter crying, "Lord, save me"
   – Matt. 14:29-30

9. Stephen "calling" and "crying"
   – Acts 7:59-60

10. Crying "Hosanna" – Matt. 21:15;
    John 12:13

11. Crying out to Jesus for mercy – Mark 10:47

12. Crying with a loud voice around the
    throne – Rev. 7:10

D. The Greek word for "crying out," "shouting," and "speaking with a strong voice"
   – *boao* (βοάω)

1. Jesus on the cross – Mark 15:34

2. John the Baptist's ministry – Matt. 3:3;
   John 1:23

3. The saints continually praying to the
   Lord for His coming back
   – Luke 18:1-8 (v. 7)

4. The release over the freedom of the new
   covenant – Gal. 4:27; Isa. 54:1 (cf. Isa.
   53—55; 12:1-6)

E. The relationship between calling and prayer
  1. Calling ushering in prayer – Jer. 29:11-13; Psa. 4:1; 55:16-17
  2. Calling when prayer doesn't work – Lam. 3:44-57
  3. Crying out in prayer – Heb. 5:7 — *krauge* (κραυγή) "crying out"

## VI. The First Mention of Calling Upon the Name of the Lord

A. God renewing and set on His original purpose ("Seth"= set /fix) – Gen. 4:25—5:2 (cf. Gen. 1:26-28)

B. Man becoming incurably sick and desperately wicked ("Enosh" = weak / frail) – Gen. 4:25-26

## VII. The History of the Experience of Calling Upon the Name of the Lord

A. Abraham – Gen. 12:8; 13:4; 21:33

B. Isaac – Gen. 26:25

C. Moses – Deut. 4:7; Psa. 99:6

D. Job – Job 12:4

E. Aaron – Psa. 99:6

F. Samson – Judg. 15:18-19

    G. Samuel – Psa. 99:6

    H. David – 2 Sam. 22:4, 7; 1 Chron. 21:26;
       Psa. 116; Matt. 22:43

    I. Elijah – 1 Kings 18:24

    J. Elisha – 2 Kings 5:11

    K. Isaiah – Isa. 12:3-4

    L. Jeremiah – Jer. 29:12; 33:2-3

    M. Joel – Joel 2:32

    N. Jonah – Jonah 1:6

    O. Zephaniah – Zeph. 3:9

    P. Zechariah – Zech. 13:9

    Q. Those who do not call upon the Lord
      – Prov. 1:28; Psa. 14:4; 53:4; 79:6;
      Hosea 7:7

## VIII. The Relationship between Calling and Our Inward Parts

    A. The regeneration of our spirit and His name
      – John 1:12-13; 3:6

    B. Calling upon the Lord as the evidence of the
      presence of life – Psa. 80:18-19

    C. The filling of our spirit and His name
      – Eph. 5:18-20; Isa. 12:3-4

    D. The things existing in our hearts become
      reality by calling upon His name – Rom.10:8-9

E. Finding Christ within you with your mouth
   – Rom. 10:6-10
F. The relationship between calling and faith
   – Rom. 10:14-17
G. Calling brings Christ into us as a gift rather
   than as a reward for our works – Rom. 10:3-17
H. Calling preserves our experience of Christ in
   the realm of grace rather than our own efforts
   – Rom. 5:17; 10:3-4, 12-13
 I. Confessing His name and the dividing of
   soul and spirit – Heb. 13:15; 3:1; 4:12-14
J. Our spirit, our speaking, and calling upon the
   name of the Lord – 2 Cor. 4:13 (cf. Psa.
   116:7-13); Job 32:18-20
K. The tongue among our members
   – James 3:2-6; Phil. 2:10-11

## IX. The Name and the Oneness of the Church

A. Gathering into His name and the oneness of
   the local church – Matt. 18:19-20
B. God's house and His name – 2 Sam. 7:13;
   1 Kings 8:16-20
C. Calling upon the name of the Lord and the
   oneness among all the churches – 1 Cor. 1:2
D. The name as the way to deal with divisions

and be brought into oneness – 1 Cor. 1:2, 10; Phil. 2:1-2; Isa. 52:6-8

E. Enjoying the name and the organic church life – Rom. 15:5-14; 14:17

F. A people for His name – Acts 15:14, 17

G. The Lord's name and His dwelling place – Deut. 12:5, 11, 21; 14:23-24; 16:2, 6, 11

H. The name, purity, and the oneness in the church – Zeph. 3:9

I. Calling and the purity of the church – 2 Tim. 2:20-22

J. The government of the church and the name – 1 Cor. 5:4

## X. Experiences of Calling Upon the Name of the Lord

A. Meeting the Lord Himself in His name – Isa. 52:6-7 (cf. Rom. 10:12-15)

B. Calling upon His name as the reality of believing – John 20:31

C. Losing the self-life and prejudices by the name – Rom. 10:12

D. Becoming inaccessibly high by His name – Psa. 20:1

E. The name releasing the nature of the life within – Acts 7:59-60

F. Calling as the way to draw water from the well of the Spirit in our spirit – Isa. 12:3-4 (cf. John 4:14)

G. Being distinguished by calling on the name – Acts 9:14, 21

H. Being dealt with by the Lord, and the name – Gen. 12:8; 13:4

I. Calling and stirring ourselves up to lay hold of the Lord – Isa. 64:6-7

J. The Spirit's use of the name against the enemy – Isa. 59:19

K. Calling to be saved from the distress of our enemies – Psa. 18:3-6

L. Calling as "deep calling unto deep" when our soul is cast down – Psa. 42:5-7

M. Calling in the day of trouble – Psa. 50:15; 86:7

N. Calling at our lowest levels – Lam. 3:54-57

O. Discovering the Lord's readiness to forgive by calling – Psa. 86:5

P. Calling as the quickest way to touch the Lord when we are in need – Psa. 102:2

Q. Calling as the way to react to our environments
   – Psa. 116:1-13; Matt. 11:25 (cf. 2 Cor. 4:13)

R. Calling and confessing His name as thanks-
   giving and praise – Psa. 116:17; Heb. 13:15

S. Calling as the way to find out how the Lord
   really feels about us – Psa. 118:5-14

T. Calling as the way to enjoy how near the
   Lord is – Psa. 145:18

U. Calling as the way to abide in the Lord
   Himself – Psa. 91:1-2, 9, 14-16

V. Calling is our response to the Lord's calling
   of us – Joel 2:32

W. Being refined and tested to be reduced to
   call on His name – Zech. 13:9

X. Experiencing the authority of His name
   – Acts 3:6, 16; 4:10, 30

Y. Calling His name and being built together in
   oneness – Zeph. 3:9

Z. The blessing of being under the name
   – Num. 6:23-27

AA. His name on our forehead – Rev. 22:4

# Scripture Index

*Old Testament*

## New Testament

Psa. 73 ; 42